VIEWPOINT

WORKBOOK 2

MICHAEL MCCARTHY

JEANNE MCCARTEN

HELEN SANDIFORD

CAMBRIDGE
UNIVERSITY PRESS

CAMBRIDGE
UNIVERSITY PRESS

32 Avenue of the Americas, New York, NY 10013-2473, USA

Cambridge University Press is part of the University of Cambridge.

It furthers the University's mission by disseminating knowledge in the pursuit of education, learning and research at the highest international levels of excellence.

www.cambridge.org
Information on this title: www.cambridge.org/9781107606319

First published 2014

Printed in Hong Kong, China, by Golden Cup Printing Company Limited

A catalog record for this publication is available from the British Library.

ISBN 978-0-521-13189-6 Student's Book
ISBN 978-1-107-60631-9 Workbook
ISBN 978-1-107-60156-7 Teacher's Edition with Assessment CD/CD-ROM
ISBN 978-1-107-66132-5 Class Audio CDs (4)
ISBN 978-1-107-67577-3 Presentation Plus
ISBN 978-1-107-65967-4 Blended Online Pack (Student's Book + Online Workbook)

Additional resources for this publication at www.cambridge.org/viewpoint

Cambridge University Press has no responsibility for the persistence or accuracy of URLs for external or third-party internet websites referred to in this publication, and does not guarantee that any content on such websites is, or will remain, accurate or appropriate. Information regarding prices, travel timetables, and other factual information given in this work is correct at the time of first printing but Cambridge University Press does not guarantee the accuracy of such information thereafter.

سرشناسه:	مکارتی، مایکل، ۱۹٤۷ - م.
	McCarthy, Michael
عنوان و نام پدیدآور:	Viewpoint: Workbook 2
مشخصات نشر:	تهران: رهنما، ۱۳۹٤ = ۲۰۱٥م.
مشخصات ظاهری:	۱۰٤ ص.: مصور، جدول.
وضعیت فهرست‌نویسی:	فیپای مختصر
یادداشت:	این مدرک در آدرس http://opac.nlai.ir قابل دسترسی است.
یادداشت:	انگلیسی.
یادداشت:	افست از روی چاپ ۲۰۱٤: دانشگاه کمبریج
آوانویسی عنوان:	ویو پوینت...
شناسه افزوده:	مکارتن، جین
شناسه افزوده:	McCarten, Jeanne
شناسه افزوده:	سندیفورد، هلن
شناسه افزوده:	Sandiford, Helen
شماره کتابشناسی ملی:	۳۷٦٦۰۸٥

Viewpoint 2 Workbook، مؤلفین: Michael McCarthy، Jeanne McCarten و Helen Sandiford، لیتوگرافی: رهنما، چاپ: چاپخانه نقره‌فام، چاپ اول: ۱۳۹٤، تیراژ: ۱۰۰۰ نسخه، ناشر: انتشارات رهنما، آدرس: مقابل دانشگاه تهران، خیابان فروردین، نبش خیابان شهدای ژاندارمری، پلاک ۱۱۲، تلفن: ۶۶٤۰۰۹۲۷، ۶۶٤۱۶۶۰٤، ۶۶٤۸۱۶۶۲، فاکس: ۶۶٤۶۷٤۲٤، فروشگاه رهنما، سعادت‌آباد، خیابان علامه طباطبایی جنوبی، بین ٤۰ و ٤۲ شرقی، پلاک ۲۹، تلفن: ۸۸۶۹٤۱۰۲، آدرس فروشگاه شماره ٤: خیابان پیروزی نبش خیابان سوم نیروی هوایی، تلفن: ۷۷٤۸۲٥۰٥، نمایشگاه کتاب رهنما، مقابل دانشگاه تهران پاساژ فروزنده، تلفن: ۶۶۹٥۰۹٥۷

قیمت: ۶۰۰۰۰ ریال

Contents

A great read

Lesson A [Grammar] Avoiding repetition 1

A **Complete the sentences with the words in the box. Use each word at least once.**

am	did	do	doesn't	haven't

1. I'm following in my siblings' footsteps. They're working hard for their degrees, and now I _____ , too.
2. My coworker is thinking about getting a different job – as I _____ . We both think it's time for a career change.
3. I've always loved new experiences and new adventures, but my best friend _____ . She prefers to stay at home and read about other people's adventures.
4. Since I had children, I haven't taken many risks in my life. My friends _____ , either – we're all comfortable with how our lives are right now.
5. I want to plan a trip to go whitewater rafting next year – my friends _____ , too. I really hope the plan works out, and I know they _____ , too.
6. I've always dreamed of becoming a professional musician. When he was younger, my brother _____ , too, but he ended up becoming a lawyer. These days, he only plays his guitar for his own enjoyment.

B **Complete the sentences with auxiliary verbs.**

1. My classmates think it's a good idea to get some work experience before they graduate. I _____ , too.
2. My sister and I decided to travel all over Europe by train last fall. She worked extra hours before our vacation so we'd have enough money. I _____ , too.
3. Have you seen the new exhibit at the museum? I haven't seen it yet, but my friend _____ . She said it's amazing.
4. Some of my classmates are struggling to complete their required courses for graduation – they're finding it tough, as I _____ .
5. I wanted to go hiking yesterday, but my friend _____ . I'm going to ask my cousin to hike with me today. I don't know if he likes hiking. Hopefully he _____ .
6. My parents have applied for a visa to emigrate to Australia, but I _____ . They really want to go soon, but I _____ . I have too many friends here.

About you **C** **Compare yourself with a friend or family member. How are your interests and daily lives the same or different?**

For example: *I've done a lot of traveling around the world, but my brother hasn't.*

_____

_____

_____

_____

_____

Lesson B Vocabulary Favorite books

A Read the blog post. Circle the best option to complete the sentences.

HOME   ABOUT ME   CONTACT ME

Share

USE YOUR OWN EXPERIENCES IN TEACHING

As an elementary school teacher, I always try to think back to my own school days before I hand out an assignment. I believe that we aren't just teaching kids reading, or math, or science – we're teaching them life skills.

Here is one memory of my school days that really **gets your head around / sticks in my mind**. In the fourth grade, my teacher told us to pick our favorite poem and **learn it by heart / lose your train of thought**. Honestly, I don't know many fourth graders that even have a favorite poem. But I chose Robert Frost's *Birches*, which is really long. There I was, ready to recite the poem, and all of a sudden I just froze. **It was on the tip of my tongue / It was beyond me**, but I just couldn't remember how it started. Eventually I remembered and recited the whole poem. And I've remembered it ever since. I can recite that poem today **come to grips with / off the top of my head**.

I know my students don't really **see the point / come to mind** of reciting poetry, especially if they **can't make head or tails of / stick in their mind** what they are saying. However, I feel like I really **learned by heart / got something out of** that activity when I was in school. At the time, I was terrified, but with each new poem I recited, I gained a bit more confidence.

It may have been a rough start, but my fourth grade teacher unwittingly paved the way for my career. Even when I **lose my train of thought / see the point**, I have no fear standing in front of a class now.

About you

B Complete the sentences with your own ideas.

1. It's beyond me why _____ .
2. Something that really sticks in my mind is _____ .
3. _____ always comes to mind when I think about my childhood.
4. I can't really see the point of _____ .
5. One thing I can't come to grips with is _____ .
6. It's easy to lose your train of thought when _____ .
7. It's very rewarding when you can get your head around _____ .
8. I've never learned _____ by heart.
9. _____ is something that I can never make heads or tails of.
10. Whenever I answer a question off the top of my head without thinking about it, _____ .

Lesson B Grammar Avoiding repetition 2

A **Read the conversations. Delete words or replace them with *one / ones*, where possible, to avoid repetition. Sometimes more than one answer is possible.**

1. *A* Do you ever read plays?
   B Yes, sometimes. The old Greek tragedies are the plays I like most.

2. *A* Did you read *To Kill a Mockingbird* in English class?
   B No, our professor said we were supposed to read *To Kill a Mockingbird*, but then we didn't have time.

3. *A* We're studying the poetry of Pablo Neruda in literature class. Have you read any of his poetry?
   B Yeah. I love it. I memorized his poetry to recite in my poetry class once.

4. *A* Do you ever read gossip magazines?
   B Well, I prefer not to read them, but sometimes if I'm waiting at the doctor's office I might look at a gossip magazine.

5. *A* My English teacher writes novels. Her last two were published.
   B Yes, I know her novels. I think her more recent novel is much better than her first novel.
   A Yeah, I agree. Actually, she's working on a new novel now.

B **Read the conversation. Delete words or replace them with *one / ones*, where possible, to avoid repetition. Sometimes more than one answer is possible.**

A I need something to read. Have you read anything good lately?

B Well, I've been reading a lot of crime novels lately. You can borrow a crime novel if you like. Do you want to borrow a crime novel?

A Thanks, but I don't like to read books about murders. I generally prefer not to read books about murders, or I get nightmares.

B OK. How about a classic like *Great Expectations*?

A Yeah, that sounds good. I've never read that classic, and I've always wanted to read that novel.

B We read it in our literature class a few years ago. Well, actually, we were supposed to read it, but I watched the movie instead.

A You did? That's funny. There are so many movies of the classics nowadays. But usually I don't watch the movie until after I've read the book, or at least I try not to watch the movie until I've read the book. Usually the books are better.

B Yeah. I have to say I usually prefer the movie. Anyway, take *Great Expectations*. Or I have some Shakespeare plays, too. I think I have most of his plays. Here, take that Shakespeare play, *Romeo and Juliet*, or *Hamlet*. You can borrow both plays if you like. I hope *Hamlet* doesn't give you nightmares, though!

A OK. Thanks.

About you

C **What kinds of books do you read? Who is your favorite author? Do you like all of his or her books? Has your taste in books changed over the years?**

_____

_____

_____

Lesson C Conversation strategies

A **Complete the conversation. Use the verbs in the box and add the auxiliary verbs *do* or *does* to add emphasis.**

appreciate	feel	make	need	think

Tamara So, Carolina, how do you like your e-reader?

Carolina Well, I have to say I _____[1] not having to carry books anymore. And I have much more room in my purse, that's for sure.

Tamara I know. I like mine, too. But it _____[2] a bit strange, you know, not turning the pages.

Carolina Is yours an older one? Like, is it in black and white? This one's in color, and it _____[3] a difference – especially if you're reading magazines and stuff.

Tamara Oh, yeah, I bet. I _____[4] a new one, actually. But you know what I like best? If I run out of things to read when I'm traveling, I can just download something.

Carolina I know. I have to say though, I haven't figured out all the functions on it yet. I _____[5] they could be easier to navigate. Like, I deleted a book the other day when I was just trying to bookmark something.

Tamara You'll get used to it soon enough.

B **Complete the conversation with *if so* or *if not*.**

Teacher OK, class, good luck with your papers, and remember, if you quote from someone's work, the references must be accurate. _____[1], you'll be penalized and get a lower grade.

Student Um, can I reference Internet blogs in my paper? And _____[2], what is the correct way to do that?

Teacher You may, but in my view simply restating one blogger's ideas is a weak, _____[3] pointless thing to do. I want to see evidence that you have consulted real authorities. As to the second question, do you have the college style guide? _____[4], you'll find all referencing information there. _____[5], you can access it on my website.

About you

C **Complete the conversations with *if so, if not,* or write the auxiliary verbs *do* or *does* to add emphasis where possible. Then answer with your own information.**

1. *A* Do you use social media sites a lot? And _____ , what do you use them for?

   B Yes, I _____ spend a lot of time on social media sites, catching up with news. And I read a lot of blogs, too. Blogs really _____ give everyone a chance to express their point of view.

   _____

2. *A* My friend just submitted a story to a publisher. She's hoping they'll publish it but _____ , she'll have to find another way to get it published. Any thoughts?

   B Well, she could publish it herself online. I mean it _____ take a little effort, but it works for some authors.

   _____

Lesson D Reading Dallas Poetry Slam – FAQs

A Prepare **What do you know about poetry slams? Check the statement you think is true. Then read the website and check your answer.**

1. They are non-competitive. _____
2. They are for professional writers only. _____
3. They combine the talent for writing poetry and performing. _____

| Home | Events | Sign-up | **FAQ** | Contact Us |

Dallas POETRY SLAM – FAQs[1]

1 **What is poetry slam?**
Simply put, poetry slam is the competitive art of performance poetry. It puts a dual emphasis on writing and performance, encouraging poets to focus on what they're saying and how they're saying it.

2 **What is a poetry slam?**
A poetry slam is a competitive event in which poets perform their work and are judged by members of the audience. Typically, the host or another organizer selects the judges, who are instructed to give numerical scores (on a 0 to 10 or 1 to 10 scale) based on the poets' content and performance.

3 **Who gets to participate?**
Slams are open to everyone who wishes to sign up and can get into the venue. Though everyone who signs up has the opportunity to read in the first round, the lineup for subsequent rounds is determined by the judges' scores. In other words, the judges vote for which poets they want to see more work from.

4 **What are the rules?**
Each poem must be of the poet's own construction. Each poet gets three minutes (plus a 10-second grace period) to read one poem. If the poet goes over time, points will be deducted from the total score. The poet may not use props, costumes, or musical instruments. Of the scores the poet receives from the five judges, the high and low scores are dropped, and the middle three are added together, giving the poet a total score of 0–30.

5 **How does it differ from an open mike[2] reading?**
Slam is engineered for the audience, whereas a number of open mike readings are engineered as a support network for poets. Slam is designed for the audience to react vocally and openly to all aspects of the show, including the poet's performance, the judges' scores, and the host's banter.

6 **What can the audience do?**
The official MC spiel of Poetry Slam, Inc., encourages the audience to respond to the poets or the judges in any way they see fit, and most slams have adopted that guideline. Audiences can boo or cheer at the conclusion of a poem, or even during a poem.

7 **What kind of poetry is read at slams?**
Depends on the venue, depends on the poets, depends on the slam. One of the best things about poetry slam is the range of poets it attracts. You'll find a diverse range of work within slam, including heartfelt love poetry, searing social commentary, uproarious comic routines, and bittersweet personal confessional pieces. Poets are free to do work in any style on any subject.

8 **How do I win a poetry slam?**
Winning a poetry slam requires some measure of skill and a huge dose of luck. The judges' tastes, the audience's reactions, and the poets' performances all shape a slam event, and what wins one week might not get a poet into the second round the next week. There's no formula for winning a slam, although you become a stronger poet and performer the same way you get to Carnegie Hall — practice, practice, practice.

SOURCE: Poetry Slam, Inc.

[1]FAQs frequently asked questions

[2]open mike a live show where audience members get up on stage, take the mike (= microphone), and perform

B Read for main ideas **Choose the correct option to complete the sentences. Write a, b, or c.**

1. In order to win a poetry slam, poets have to focus on _____ .
   a. their poetry writing skills
   b. the delivery of their poem
   c. both a and b

2. The judges at a poetry slam are chosen by _____ .
   a. the audience
   b. an event official
   c. the poets

3. All participants at a poetry slam have to _____ .
   a. read a number of poems
   b. read their own poem
   c. read classic poetry

4. A slam is different from an open mike because _____ .
   a. an open mike event focuses on entertaining the audience
   b. a slam is designed to provide support for young poets
   c. the audience's reaction is what matters most

5. At a slam, audience members _____ .
   a. might show support and cheer for the performers
   b. are asked to calm down if they react too loudly
   c. both a and b

6. One of the unique things about poetry slams is _____ .
   a. that the audience can determine the theme for the event
   b. all of the poems for an event focus on one topic
   c. it includes many different types of poetry

7. To win poetry slams, you need _____ .
   a. to be a consistently strong performer
   b. to gauge the audience's reaction, amongs other things
   c. nothing more than a big dose of luck

C Read for detail **Are the sentences true or false, or is the information not given on the webpage? Write T, F, or NG. Correct the false sentences.**

1. At a poetry slam, poets receive a score for their performance. _____
2. The performers at a poetry slam have all been invited to participate. _____
3. Poetry slams started 10 years ago. _____
4. A poet can read a poem that he / she did not write. _____
5. Performers get penalized for spending too much time on one poem. _____
6. A poet can use any items during the performance to enhance their reading. _____
7. Poetry slams are becoming more popular than open mike readings. _____
8. Poems on political issues are not allowed at poetry slams. _____

About
you

D React **Answer the questions with your own opinions.**

1. Would you like to go to a poetry slam? Why?

_____

_____

2. What characteristics do you think a person needs to be successful at a poetry slam?

_____

_____

Writing A book review

A Underline the linked adjectives in the book review.

A dark yet thrilling novel, Fyodor Dostoevsky's *Crime and Punishment* focuses on the psychological aspects of murder. Published in 1866, the novel describes how the main character, Raskolnikov, plans and executes a murder and deals with the resulting guilt. Raskolnikov is a thoughtful though arrogant character. His arrogance prompts him to commit a terrible, even brutal, crime to prove his superiority.

Throughout the novel, Dostoevsky builds a tense, dramatic chain of events by simultaneously describing the criminal investigation and Raskolnikov's psychological state. His internal suffering eventually comes to an unpredictable though perhaps realistic resolution. Readers of *Crime and Punishment* may find it a disturbing, if not depressing, work. However, it does provide the reader with an insight into the innermost thoughts of a criminal. As a whole, it is considered one of the best examples of nineteenth century Russian literature.

B Circle the best option to complete the sentences from a review of *Crime and Punishment*.

1. *Crime and Punishment* is a long **yet / or even** action-packed novel, filled with a number of unexpected events.
2. At the beginning of the book, we see a cold **, / yet** detached young man planning a crime he feels he has every right to commit.
3. After committing the crime, his confused **and / if** desperate actions reflect his guilt about the murder.
4. Things start to turn against him when he rants about the crime to a concerned **yet / if not** suspicious official.
5. The official's clever, **even / but** insightful plan is to make Raskolnikov worry so much about being caught that he eventually confesses.
6. A nervous **but / and** anxious Raskolnikov eventually confesses to his crime.

C Editing **Correct the mistakes in the coordinated adjectives, but do not use *and*. More than one answer is possible. One sentence is correct.**

1. Dostoevsky's novels are complex yet difficult.
2. His work has often been described as thought-provoking philosophical.
3. The vocabulary in the book is rich, at times obscure.
4. It forces us to ask some difficult if not impossible questions about ourselves.
5. Readers may find the initial plot development slow, boring.
6. For me, reading a Dostoevsky novel is an intriguing though fascinating experience.
7. However, his novels can leave the reader feeling saddened but depressed.

D Think of a book you have enjoyed that has memorable characters. Write a review evaluating both the story and the characters. Check your work for errors.

Listening extra A young novelist

A Imagine you want to become a published author. Which three things would you try to do?

_____ Start by writing a blog on the Internet.
_____ Try to publish a story in a school or student newspaper.
_____ Attend a writer's workshop.
_____ Perform at a poetry slam.
_____ Self-publish an e-book.
_____ Try to get accepted to a writers' conference.
_____ Take a creative writing class.
_____ Share your ideas for a book with your friends.
_____ Ask established authors to edit your work.

B [icon] **Listen to the radio interview with Rebecca Jackson. Check (✔) the things from Exercise A that she tried doing to get published.**

C [icon] **Listen again. Are the sentences true or false? Write T or F.**

1. _2050_ is Rebecca's first novel. _____
2. Rebecca's professor did not have any advice for aspiring writers. _____
3. Rebecca received an "A" in her creative writing class. _____
4. Despite her setbacks, Rebecca's urge to communicate with people kept her motivated. _____
5. Rebecca's parents thought it was a good idea for her to take a year off school. _____
6. Rebecca heard about self-published e-books at a poetry slam event. _____

D [icon] **Listen again and complete the sentences.**

1. Rebecca is _____ years old.
2. She took a creative writing class during her _____ year in college.
3. Her short story was rejected from the _____ _____ .
4. Rebecca loved the idea of e-books because she wouldn't have to contend with large, _____ publishers.
5. Jenny Davis, the main character in _2050_, is a shy _____ young woman.
6. The host of the radio show describes the main character as soft-spoken yet rather _____ .

About you

E **Answer the questions with your own opinions.**

1. If you wanted to publish a book, would you publish it yourself, or would you try to get it published by a big publisher? Why?

_____

_____

2. Will the ability for people to publish their own e-books mean more great books getting published, or will it mean more uninteresting books by bad authors?

_____

_____

Now complete the _Unit 1 Progress chart_ on page 98.

Technology

Lesson A Grammar Adding information to nouns

A **Replace the underlined relative clauses with other types of phrases. Sometimes more than one answer is possible.**

ONLINE PRIVACY: A Generational Divide

By Dr. Jane Thomas

Recently I had my sociology class read an article about online privacy and security.

In my opinion, online privacy is a topic that should be taken[1] very seriously. Therefore I devoted an entire class period to the topic. I thought students would be surprised to discover how advertisers create ads for each consumer that are based on data[2] they have collected[3] from previous purchases or product searches. I anticipated that they would be disturbed to learn about programs that are designed to search[4] for keywords in your emails in order to target advertising. However, to my surprise, the students who are in my class[5] did not seem at all concerned about online privacy and security. In fact, some students who were no doubt hoping to reassure me[6] noted that it is sometimes beneficial to see advertisements that are directly targeted[7] to their needs and interests. Many of my students said that adjusting the settings which are on their account[8] provides a sense of security.

When I asked them how they would feel about random people who live around the world[9] viewing all their photos and other personal information on social networking sites, many of them reported that this idea was not something that they need to worry about[10]. For my students, personal information is something that can be shared[11]. By the end of the class, I concluded that my students' views on online security were yet another example of the generational divide that exists[12] between those who grew up with technology and those who didn't.

1. _to be taken_
2. _____
3. _____
4. _____
5. _____
6. _____
7. _____
8. _____
9. _____
10. _____
11. _____
12. _____

About you

B **Complete the questions with correct forms of the verbs given. Then answer the questions. Give reasons for your answers.**

1. What do you think about websites _____ (display) ads for items _____ (base) on similar items you have looked at online?

2. Do you think email messages _____ (provide) coupons based on your recent purchases are something _____ (welcome), or are they an invasion of privacy _____ (condemn)?

3. Are you concerned about social networking sites _____ (program) to share your personal information with advertisers? Why or why not?

Lesson B Vocabulary Compound adjectives

A Complete the blog post with the expressions in the box. There is one extra expression.

air-conditioned	energy-efficient	home-cooked	self-cleaning
climate-controlled	high-speed	last-minute	solar-powered

HOME   MY TRAVELS   ABOUT ME   CONTACT ME

Do you want to get away from it all? GO LOW-TECH!

Goodbye vacation   I'm sure you've had this same experience: You plan a vacation, but you end up working during your time off. You arrive to find yourself stuck in an _____¹ room, instead of enjoying the fresh air and tropical temperatures on the beach. You feel obligated to answer emails because you have access to the hotel's _____² Internet. And just when you finally think you are free, your boss makes a _____³ request! Goodbye vacation! Sound familiar?

Time to go low-tech!   I have worked during one too many vacations. So this year, I decided to go completely low-tech. I stayed in a bungalow on the beach. There was no Internet or cell service. I went in the summer, but the room was _____⁴ with the sea breezes through the open windows. The water heater for the shower was _____⁵, which is perfect for a place that is sunny most of the year. These are true examples of _____⁶ accommodations!

I ate delicious _____⁷ meals prepared by the owners. They were fantastic! So, next time you are planning a vacation, go low-tech, and get away from it all.

B Complete the discussion with the expressions in the box. There is one extra expression.

carbon-neutral	custom-built	human-like	labor-saving	last-minute

Host   OK. Let's take some questions from the audience. Yes, sir, what's your question?

Man   Um, is it your intention to create a robot that not only looks like a regular person, but is also _____¹ in other ways?

Professor   Well, at this point, we're trying to make certain jobs less time-consuming, so we see robots as _____² devices. We don't imagine they'll have more caring human qualities.

Woman   I'd like to ask, when you assemble robots, are they always _____³ for particular customers? I mean, do people order them for their own purposes?

Professor   It depends on the customer. We usually try to tackle several problems at once.

Woman   And how about the cost of running a robot? Do they use a lot of energy?

Professor   Actually, we've also been working on an eco-friendly robot that is _____⁴.

About you **C** Imagine you could have a custom-built robot. What would it be like? Would it be human-like? Energy-efficient? What labor-saving chores would it do? Write a paragraph.

Lesson B   Grammar   Combining ideas

A Complete the article with the conjunctions *both . . . and, either . . . or, neither . . . nor,* and *not only . . . but also.* Sometimes there is more than one correct answer.

MASDAR CITY

In 2008, construction began on the first sustainable city in the world, known as Masdar City. Located 11 miles (17 kilometers) outside of Abu Dhabi in the United Arab Emirates, Masdar City is designed to be an eco-friendly urban environment. The city depends ____not only____[1] on renewable energy sources, _____[2] aims to create a zero-waste ecology. Consequently, _____[3] gas-powered cars _____[4] equipment that uses fossil fuels are permitted within the city limits. City planners designed the city to provide two easy forms of transportation. Residents can _____[5] walk _____[6] take driverless electric vehicles all around this modern landscape. Masdar City has given city planners around the globe _____[7] a model for a high-tech; sustainable city _____[8] new insights into creating energy-efficient living spaces.

B Rewrite the sentences using the conjunctions in parentheses.

1. Masdar City relies on technological innovation. It also draws on traditional Arabic architecture. (not only . . . but also) _Masdar City not only relies on technological innovation, but it also draws on traditional Arabic architecture_ .

2. In Masdar City, solar power will be used to generate energy. Wind farms will also be used. (both . . . and) _____ _____ .

3. Biological waste will not be thrown away. Industrial waste will also not be thrown away. (neither . . . nor) _____ _____ .

4. The completion of Masdar City will be in 2020. It might be in 2025. (either . . . or) _____ _____ .

5. The walls surrounding the city were designed to keep out gas-powered cars. They were also designed for protection from the hot, desert winds. (not only . . . but also) _____ _____ .

6. Clean-tech companies are expected to occupy some of the city's buildings. Major research institutes are also expected to occupy some of the buildings. (both . . . and) _____ _____ .

7. According to the plans, wastewater will be used for crop irrigation. It could also be used to maintain the city's parks. (either . . . or) _____ _____ .

About you

C Describe your ideal city. What would make it more innovative and high-tech than where you live now? Use conjunctions to explain your ideas.

_____
_____
_____

Lesson C Conversation strategies

A Circle the best options to complete the conversation.

Victoria Sorry I'm late. I was walking out the door when Sara called. She got into a car accident a few hours ago.

Yarah Oh, no! Really? Is she OK?

Victoria Yeah. Thankfully, she's fine and no one else was involved. **Predictably / Invariably**, she was talking on her hands-free headset and driving at the same time. She **ideally / evidently** got distracted and hit a tree on the side of the road.

Yarah You're kidding! I've told her a million times it's not a good idea to drive and talk on the phone at the same time. Even if she is wearing her headset.

Victoria I know. I know. I've told her that multitasking is **potentially / ironically** dangerous when you're driving.

Yarah Well, **apparently / ideally** she didn't listen to either one of us.

Victoria I guess not. But you know how some people are – they **ideally / inevitably** stick to their bad habits.

Yarah True. Luckily she didn't get hurt. **Ideally / Evidently**, she'll learn her lesson from this. I mean, she can't possibly think it's OK to drive and talk on the phone after today!

B Complete the conversation with the expressions in the box. Use one expression twice.

can't possibly	couldn't possibly	evidently	ideally	ironically	potentially

A Um, you know we have a test tomorrow, right? You _____[1] be studying and texting at the same time!

B Oh, this is nothing! I could _____[2] watch TV, too, and still concentrate.

A Seriously? If I were you, I _____[3] get anything done. _____[4], that's not a problem for you. I mean, you don't do your homework like this every day, do you?

B Well, yeah. Multitasking just works for me, and _____[5] I seem to do even better when I do several things at once.

A I guess it's possible. But according to an article I read, people _____[6] focus on more than one thing at a time. It also said that _____[7] you should work in a *totally* quiet room without any distractions.

About you

C Complete the sentences with your own ideas.

1. I can't possibly _____ and _____ at the same time.
2. Ideally, when I am studying, I _____ .
3. I think it is potentially dangerous to _____ .
4. Predictably, I get good grades when _____ .
5. I try to stay healthy by _____ . Supposedly, _____ is good for you.
6. I couldn't possibly _____ while I was watching TV.
7. Invariably, if I'm daydreaming in class, the teacher _____ .
8. Apparently, I'm in a better mood and easier to get along with when _____ .

Lesson D Reading E-books

A **Prepare** **How do you think e-books have affected reading habits and book sales? Write three guesses. Then read the article to see if your ideas are mentioned.**

E-books spur reading among Americans, survey shows

1   E-books aren't just becoming increasingly popular. They also appear to be promoting reading habits among American adults. So says new research from the Pew Internet and American Life Project, which states that about one-fifth of U.S. adults have read an e-book in the past year.

2   And if you expand that to include Americans over 16 who have used an e-reader device or app to read news articles or magazine-style features, the figure jumps to 43 percent.

3   E-book users tend to read more often than people who read only print material, Pew found. In particular, they read more books. A typical e-book user read 24 books in the past year, compared with the 15 books reported by typical non-e-book users.

4   Also, a third of people who read e-content say they now spend more time reading than they did before e-books. This is especially true for people who own tablets and e-book readers.

5   This might be good for the economy. According to Pew, e-book users are "also more likely than others to have bought their most recent book, rather than borrowed it, and they are more likely than others to say they prefer to purchase books in general."

6   E-readers and tablets (including Amazon's Kindle Fire e-reader, which is a modified Android tablet) were a popular holiday gift item last year. Currently 28 percent of Americans age 18 and older own at least one tablet or an e-book reader. And that's not even counting the people who read books on a smartphone or iPod Touch app.

7   Then again, Pew also noted that e-book users often start searching for books online — which isn't great news for people who run brick-and-mortar bookstores.

8   For now, print reading material still rules the consumer market, however. Pew found that nearly three-fourths of U.S. adults read a printed book in 2011, and 11 percent listened to an audio book. Print books are especially popular when people read to children.

9   Print books are also the most popular choice when people want to borrow or lend a book. That's not surprising — recently author Dave Taylor explained step-by-step how to borrow a Kindle book from a public library. It's not too difficult, but is still considerably more complicated than walking into the library and pulling a book off the shelf.

10   The survey also found that just slightly more people prefer e-books over print for reading in bed.

11   On the flip side, Pew noted that nearly 20 percent of U.S. adults said they had not read a single book in the past year. In general, people who don't own electronic reading devices are more likely not to read much at all.

12   In addition, nearly 20 percent of Americans 16 and older said they had "physical or health conditions that made reading difficult or challenging." Most of these people are older (25 percent of those over age 50), unemployed, or low-income. But an interesting aspect of e-book and audio book technology is its potential to improve the accessibility of written content.

13   Most e-reading devices allow the reader to adjust the font, font size, contrast, column width, and other factors to compensate for impaired vision. Plus, they often include text-to-speech technology that can read books or articles aloud — maybe not with thrilling delivery, but still a useful option. This can also be helpful to people with limited literacy.

14   The cost of e-reading devices keeps dropping, and it's likely that in the next year or two companies like Amazon may be giving away basic e-readers for free (on the principle that you can make more money selling "blades" than "razors").

15   As the price of e-readers approaches zero, it opens up more opportunities for people who have been left on the wrong side of the digital divide to access the same wealth of information, entertainment, and education as people with normal vision and average-or-better income.

16   Since the invention of writing, the written word has always disrupted the balance of power in societies. While e-books might have started out as a high-tech novelty for early adopters, they may ultimately prove to be a great equalizer across boundaries of ability, resources, and education.

SOURCE: www.cnn.com

B Read for main ideas **Read the article again. Check (✔) the true statements.**

☐ People who read e-books read more often than those who read print books.
☐ The majority of Americans under 18 own e-readers.
☐ The development of e-books has created economic problems for traditional bookstores.
☐ E-readers were still too expensive to be a popular gift for the holidays last year.
☐ People who read to children prefer print books to e-books.

C Paraphrase **Write the number of the paragraphs next to each description.**

1. The growing popularity of e-books may be affecting sales at bookstores. _____
2. The cost of e-readers means that more people with lower incomes can enjoy what e-books have to offer. _____
3. E-books may remove social, educational, and physical limitations, just as written word changed the balance of social powers. _____
4. E-book users are avid readers, more so than readers of print books. _____ , _____
5. Book sales have gone up because e-book users like to buy rather than borrow books. _____
6. E-books help those who have trouble reading due to certain disabilities. _____
7. Print books are more typically lent and borrowed. _____
8. E-readers have recently become a popular holiday gift. _____

D Read for details **Answer the questions. Check (✔) a, b, or c.**

1. According to the article, why are e-readers good for the economy?
   ☐ a. People buy more content to read.
   ☐ b. People go to more bookstores.
   ☐ c. People buy the e-book and the print book.
2. Why are print books more popular with people who go to the library?
   ☐ a. People find it easier to borrow a print book from the library.
   ☐ b. It's cheaper.
   ☐ c. both a and b
3. What is the principle that is driving companies to consider giving e-readers away?
   ☐ a. They can make more money by selling e-books than by selling the e-reading devices.
   ☐ b. They want readers with lower incomes to read more.
   ☐ c. They can ensure that customers will never buy print books again.
4. How are e-readers helping to bridge the digital divide?
   ☐ a. They are becoming so easy to operate that anyone can use one.
   ☐ b. They are attracting a wider audience because more e-books are being published.
   ☐ c. Their low cost means everyone can have access to information.

About you

E React **Answer the questions with your own opinions.**

1. What did you find most interesting about the article? Did anything surprise you?

   _____

   _____

2. Is the information in the article also true about people you know? In what way?

   _____

   _____

3. Do you prefer e-readers or print books? Why?

   _____

   _____

Writing Describing graphs, charts, and tables

A Look at the table. Then circle the best options to complete the article.

Internet access by age and location
2011 United States of America Census Data

Age	Total adults	At home	At work	At school or a library
18 to 34 years old	30.48	33.34	31.74	58.92
35 to 54 years old	37.77	41.31	50.09	29.93
55 years old and over	31.75	25.35	18.18	11.16

The table **shows / accounted for** where Americans accessed the Internet in 2010. As **accounted for / can be seen** in the table, 41.31 percent of 35 to 54 year olds used the Internet at home **as compared to / as shown** only 25.35 percent of those older than 55. **In comparison, / In contrast to** all other age groups, 58.92 percent of 18 to 34 year olds used the Internet at school or the library. Just over half of 35 to 54 year olds used the Internet at work, **accounted for / in comparison to** a third of 18 to 34 year olds and less than 20 percent of people 55 and over.

B Complete the sentences about the table above using the expressions in the box. Use capital letters where necessary.

> accounted   as can be seen in   illustrates   in comparison with   in contrast   represented

1. The table _____ where people of different ages access the Internet.
2. _____ other age groups, those 55 years and older were less likely to go online at work.
3. However, the 55 years and over age group was least likely to use a library or school, which _____ for only 11.16 percent of that age group's place of Internet access.
4. The workplace _____ the most popular location for Internet access in the age group 35 to 54 years.
5. _____ the table, about a third of 18 to 34 year olds had Internet access at home.
6. _____ , just over a quarter of the older age group had Internet access at home.

C Editing **Correct the mistakes. There is one error in each sentence.**

1. As it can be seen in the graph, the number of people using smartphones has increased.
2. In 2010, the number of Americans owning cell phones represented for 85 percent of the total population.
3. China has the highest number of Internet users, in comparison other countries.
4. According to the Pew Internet and American Life Project, e-book users read 24 books per year, compared print book readers, who only read 15 books per year.
5. In the past, a small group of "innovators," who accounted to two percent of consumers, were the first to buy hi-tech products.
6. As it is shown in the graph, the number of people who use the Internet on their phones has doubled.

D Write a report on the table in Exercise A. Use expressions for describing and comparing information.

Listening extra   The hazards of e-waste

A **For each topic below, predict one fact that you would expect to hear about in a documentary about e-waste (old electronic equipment that is thrown away).**

☐ cell phones and computers: <u>They end up in landfill sites.</u>
_____

☐ consumers who buy electronics: _____
_____

☐ oceans around the world: _____
_____

☐ possible health problems: _____
_____

☐ environmental problems: _____
_____

☐ animals and birds: _____
_____

☐ recycling: _____
_____

B Listen to the documentary. Check the topics in Exercise A that are discussed.

C Listen again. Are the sentences true or false? Write T or F.

1. Most consumers know what happens to their cell phones and laptops when they discard them. _____
2. All the possible health dangers from e-waste are known. _____
3. E-waste is often shipped to recycling centers in developing countries and taken apart. _____
4. Workers in recycling centers are always given protective clothing. _____
5. Exposure to lead can cause problems with the central nervous system. _____
6. The amount of e-waste produced is not expected to rise in the next few years. _____
7. Toxic chemicals from e-waste can get into groundwater supplies. _____
8. So far, regulation of e-waste has not been completely successful. _____

D Listen to part of the documentary again. Answer the questions using the numbers in the box. There are two extra.

15–20%	50%	80–85%	20 million	30 million	50 million

1. How many tons of e-waste are produced every year? _____
2. How many computers does the U.S. throw away every year? _____
3. How much e-waste is reported as being recycled now? _____
4. How much e-waste goes to landfills each year? _____

About you

E **Answer the questions with your opinions.**

1. What do you think electronics companies can do to limit the amount of e-waste produced?
_____
_____

2. What do you think countries can or should do to deal with the issue of e-waste?
_____
_____

Now complete the *Unit 2 Progress chart* on page 98.

Society

Lesson A **Grammar** Linking events

A **Complete the conversation with the participles in the box.**

bearing	growing up	having worried	not being	speaking

Mark I don't understand why my friends need to replace their cell phones and tablets and stuff every year. I mean, _____[1] in sort of a poor family, I was taught never to spend money if I didn't absolutely have to.

Laura Yeah, but there's a lot of social pressure these days. I mean, _____[2] as someone who's bought four new cell phones in three years, I am obviously totally unable to resist the pressure.

Mark . Well, _____[3] able to afford constant upgrades, I just try to be happy with what I have.

Laura But you could afford it if you decided it was a priority. I mean, _____[4] in mind how much people use technology, you have to keep up in some jobs.

Mark Yeah. I know. But _____[5] about it for some time, I've now decided I don't care if my stuff looks a little old fashioned. I'd rather spend my money on other things.

B **Rewrite the article by replacing the underlined words with participle clauses. Delete unnecessary words and add punctuation if needed.**

Do you feel pressured to buy the latest gadgets?

Natalie Sherman, SENIOR: "<u>I come from a family that didn't have a lot of money, so</u> I couldn't have all the things I wanted. As a teenager, I often felt embarrassed <u>because I never had the same phone as my friends.</u> I don't feel that way anymore."

<u>Coming from a family that didn't have a lot of money, I couldn't have all the things I wanted.</u>

_____

_____

_____

Armando Lopez, FRESHMAN: "<u>I grew up in a low-tech home, and</u> I never felt the need to have all the latest technology. These days, <u>I live in a university environment</u>, so I feel much more pressure to keep up. And you know what? <u>Because I don't want to look like I'm totally behind the times,</u> yesterday I went out and spent a fortune on a new phone!"

_____

_____

_____

_____

_____

Chung-hee Park, JUNIOR: "<u>I'm a communications major, so</u> I need to buy the latest phones, gadgets, apps, etc. <u>I've thought about it, and</u> I've stopped worrying about all the money I'm spending. I think of it as an education expense."

_____

_____

_____

_____

_____

About you **C** **Answer the question from the article with your own information.**

_____

_____

Lesson B Vocabulary New experiences

A Circle the best options to complete the *take* expressions in the post on a college website.

HOME   ABOUT   ACADEMICS   ADMISSIONS   COMMUNITY / CULTURE   ATHLETICS   **ASK QUESTIONS**   QUICK LINKS

I'm a freshman on a scholarship, and I'm so worried about my grades that I've been avoiding most social activities. It's making me a little depressed. Any suggestions? — LonelyFreshman asked - 27 minutes ago

I'm a sophomore now, but I know how you're feeling. In my freshman year, I wanted to do well, so I let my studies take **note of / precedence over** everything else. Whenever there were a lot of people around the dorm, I took **refuge / steps** in the library. My grades were pretty good, but I hadn't taken **into account / for granted** just how lonely I would feel. Finally, I took **precedence over / stock of** things and decided I needed to take **credit for / advantage of** some of the extracurricular activities here. Actually, it was my roommate who took **charge of / advantage of** the situation. He encouraged me to take **part in / stock of** some sports activities with him. And he can also take **credit for / note of** getting me involved in co-ed volleyball! Getting exercise and making friends makes me feel better, and my grades have actually gone up! — JB2020 - 10 minutes ago

B Complete the article with the *take* expressions in the box.

take advantage	take into account	take refuge	take steps	take time
take for granted	take note	take responsibility	take the initiative	

FIRST TRIP ABROAD?   Some dos and don'ts for the novice traveler

Before any trip, there are several _____ that you should _____ to prepare.

- Even if you're going on a guided tour, _____ for learning about the country before you go. Read about the country's history, cultural heritage, and social customs.

- Don't _____ that everyone you meet will understand English. Learn important phrases like "Hello," "Good-bye," "I'm sorry," and "Thank you" in the local language.

When you arrive, keep in mind the following things:

- Make sure you visit the most important museums and monuments, but also _____ each day to walk around the streets and spend an hour or so exploring the shops, markets, and local architecture.

- As you explore, _____ of the local customs so that you can behave or dress appropriately.

- If you feel people aren't being polite to you, remember to _____ that different cultures don't always follow the same rules. What seems rude in one country may actually be polite in another.

- If you know the local language, _____ to talk to servers and sales personnel in shops and stores. If you don't speak up first, they may address you in your own language and you'll lose the opportunity to practice.

- Be sure to get an early start each day, but don't be afraid to _____ in your hotel room when you feel really tired. You need to feel rested in order to _____ of all the wonderful things the culture has to offer.

About you   **C** Answer the questions with your own information. Use the underlined expressions.

1. Have you <u>taken part in</u> any new activities this year? _____

_____

2. What <u>takes precedence</u> in your life these days – your studies (or job) or your social activities?

_____

3. Have you ever <u>taken</u> something or someone <u>for granted</u> and then regretted it later?

_____

Lesson B Grammar Adding emphasis

A Circle the best options to complete the article on a website for young entrepreneurs.

As a young entrepreneur, I've had to face many challenges. The first was to convince people that I needed to drop out of college in order to start my own business. My parents were **such / so** upset that we barely spoke for months. **Even / Only** my best friend thought it was a bad idea. I finally realized that **only / even** I could make the decision, and so I went ahead with my plans. The second challenge was to find time for a social life. Building a business from the ground up was **such / so** hard work that I didn't **only / even** have the energy to go out for coffee with friends. A different sort of challenge came from the fact that I was **so / such** young, since some of my potential clients didn't think I was old enough to take on **such / only** a huge responsibility. I remember one of them saying, "You're **only / even** a college kid – how can you possibly be running a company?" Remarks like that were **such / so** discouraging that I wondered at times if I had made the wrong decision. Ultimately, though, I was just **such / so** committed to building a successful business that I refused to give up.

B Rewrite each pair of sentences as a single sentence, using *so . . . that* or *such . . . that*. Delete unnecessary words and add punctuation if needed.

1. Starting a new job is often a stressful experience. Even the most self-confident person can get nervous.

    Starting a new job is such a stressful experience that even the most self-confident
    person can get nervous.

2. Learning new skills can be a very demanding task. New employees often feel overwhelmed.

    _____

    _____

3. Employees are often embarrassed about not knowing something. As a result, they're afraid to ask for help.

    _____

    _____

4. Understanding a company's culture is a very important part of fitting in. Therefore, new employees need to make it a major priority.

    _____

    _____

5. Most employees eventually become very comfortable in their jobs. So they completely forget how hard things were in the beginning.

    _____

    _____

Lesson C Conversation strategies

A Complete the conversation with the words in the box.

again	but	having	so	then	though

Angela I read this article yesterday where the author says women shouldn't wait too long before starting a family. She says they should have their children when they're in their early twenties.

Tamara Wow. That's the opposite of what's happening in a lot of places. But then _____¹, maybe she has a point. It's easier to adapt to a big change in lifestyle when you're young.

Angela That's true. But even _____², if a woman doesn't take a job right out of college, she may ruin her chances of having a career. _____³ said that, _____⁴, it's probably less risky for the baby.

Tamara Yeah, I've heard that the older the parents are, the more likely it is there'll be problems.

Angela Right, _____⁵ then there's the issue of maturity. That's why so many people don't get married until they're in their thirties.

Tamara Yeah, and even _____⁶ some people don't seem mature enough to take on such a huge responsibility!

B Complete the conversation with contrasting views. Write the letters a–f.

> a. life was very difficult for average people
> b. I guess it's not that clear right now what's going to happen in the future
> c. people's lives were just much simpler
> d. in some ways I think opportunities are shrinking for lots of people
> e. your grandfather probably didn't have as many opportunities as we have today
> f. they don't have much job security

Roberto I often think life used to be a lot less complicated years ago.

Sam Well, yeah, but then again, _____¹. I mean, they had to work harder and had less free time.

Roberto Maybe, but even so, _____² – not easier, but simpler. Probably because people had fewer choices to make. Take my grandfather, for example. After he graduated from college, he immediately got a good job, started a family, and stayed at the same company for 40 years.

Sam OK, so that sounds like a stable life. But then again, _____³. In today's world, maybe he would have had a more exciting life.

Roberto That's probably true. Even so, _____⁴. I mean, nowadays people have to work hard to land a good job. And even then, _____⁵. Companies are going out of business all the time.

Sam Oh, that's just a temporary situation. You know, the economy is changing so fast with the Internet and all. But, having said that, _____⁶.

About you **C** Complete the sentences with your own ideas.

1. They say it's better to start a family early in life. But then again, _____
_____

2. Life might be easier in some ways than it was in the past. Having said that, though, _____
_____

3. Young people today face more challenges than ever before. Even so, _____
_____

Lesson D Reading English and the Internet

A **Prepare** **All of the following expressions owe their existence to the Internet. How many other examples can you think of?**

| an app | to blog | to friend someone | a pop-up ad | to scroll down |

B **Read the article. How many words from the article had you thought of in Exercise A?**

THE CHANGING LANGUAGE OF THE INTERNET

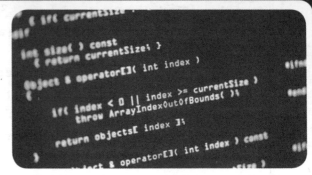

1 Since its commercial explosion in the 1990s, the Internet has radically changed many aspects of our lives – the way we shop, how we communicate with each other, where we find out information, and, in some cases, where we work. It is even changing our very language, subtly but with great rapidity.

HOW THE INTERNET CHANGED THE ENGLISH LANGUAGE

2 Even the word "Internet" has changed since its inception. While once upon a time spelling out the word with anything other than a capital "I" at the front would earn you a sharp reproach for failing to address a proper noun with the respect it deserved, these days it is more acceptable to use a lowercase "i," denoting a common noun. Why? Possibly because the Internet was once a more definitive object in its own right, referring to a tangible network of computers, whereas today the Internet has become a more abstract concept referring to the jumbled multitudes of information that can be found online.

3 Similarly, a "web site" (as in, a site on the Web) formed a new compound noun long ago to become "website." This is just one example of the internet creating new language to describe the objects that exist within its virtual realms.

4 In many cases, the jury is still out on the specifics of these new terminologies that have been thrust into the English language, in many cases transitioning from buzzwords to everyday words within the click of a mouse.

5 "Electronic mail," once a wonderfully exotic signifier of a brave new age, has since become a word used casually dozens of times a day in offices and homes throughout the world. Since becoming a commonly used term, electronic mail has also become a compound noun, using only the first letter of the adjective part. But even some dictionaries differ on the specifics, and forms of the word commonly seen include E-Mail, e-mail, E-mail, and email.

BLOGGERS BLOGGING ON THEIR BLOGS

6 "Blog" too has become a commonly used word in everyday conversation and serious journalism, to the extent that it's easy to forget it is a relatively recent blend, or portmanteau, of "web log." What's more, it's even given birth to its own verbs, i.e., "blogging" and "blog," and descriptive terms for people who indulge in such activities ("bloggers").

7 Google, meanwhile, is an impressive example of a proper noun that has become a verb synonymous with searching the Internet (to "google" something), within little more than a decade.

8 Even more recently, social networks have brought yet more neologisms to the table, and these days people are so busy "tweeting," "digging," and "friending," you'd be excused for mistaking the Internet for some sort of bizarre loved-up hippy commune.

9 Like it or not, the Internet is changing the way we use language at a tremendous pace. Once upon a time, new words would take decades or more to embed themselves in common use and dictionaries. Whereas today's instantaneous global communications mean the English language is very much at the mercy of whatever happens to be "trending" at the time.

SOURCE: www.writemysite.co.uk

C Read for main ideas **Choose the correct option to complete the sentences.**

1. The Internet is changing the English language _____ .
   a. in negative ways
   b. quickly
   c. extremely slowly
2. The author states that the word "internet" is often no longer capitalized because it now refers to _____ .
   a. a physical network of computers
   b. an abstract collection of online information
   c. a single, central computer
3. The word *blog* is an example of _____ .
   a. two words combined as one
   b. a foreign word
   c. an old word with a new meaning
4. An example of a name that people now use as a verb is _____ .
   a. blog
   b. google
   c. friend
5. Social networks have led to the creation of words such as _____ .
   a. *tweeting* and *friending*
   b. *hippy* and *loved-up*
   c. *googling* and *blogging*
6. Years ago, it took _____ for new words to appear in dictionaries.
   a. longer
   b. less time
   c. the same amount of time

D Guess words in context **Replace the words in bold with words and expressions from the article that have the same meanings.**

1. New words relating to the Internet are being added to the English language with great **speed**. (para. 1)
2. In the past, forgetting to use a capital letter might have received **harsh criticism**. (para. 2)
3. In many cases, **there is no definitive decision** on how to spell new Internet terms. (para. 4)
4. Many Internet terms began as **fashionable expressions** used by a select group of people. (para. 5)
5. The verb *google* now **means the same as** "search the Internet." (para. 7)
6. Dictionaries are rapidly adding many **newly created words** related to the Internet. (para. 7)
7. The English language is **extremely dependent on** the various websites and whatever is **being talked or written about** on the Internet. (para. 9)

About you

E React **Answer the questions with your own ideas and opinions.**

1. How has technology, such as cell phones and laptops, affected your writing?

   _____

   _____

2. Do you think linguists should be worried about new words entering the lexicon? Why or why not?

   _____

   _____

3. What new words have entered your language as a result of the Internet and social media?

   _____

   _____

Writing Writing an evaluation

A Circle the correct option to complete the evaluation.

The following is an evaluation of the Summer Intensive Program in Wildlife Conservation. In this report I will comment on the classroom instruction and the field trips, and I will conclude by offering a general recommendation.

The teachers in the program demanded a lot from the students. **Consequently, / Even so,** the students had to work extremely hard to meet their high standards. **In spite of / Because of** all the hard work required, we gained detailed knowledge of ecosystems and good conservation practices. The classes were lively with lots of teacher-student interaction, **giving / so** everyone the opportunity to participate. **Consequently / As a result of** the interactive teaching styles, all of the students got really involved in the classes.

The field trips, on the other hand, were not as well organized. Often the bus rides were **such / so** long that we did not have enough time to explore the habitats we were studying. In addition, some tour guides presented **so / such** detailed information that students felt overwhelmed. **Having said that, / As a result,** the field trips gave us a unique opportunity to observe wildlife that we had never seen before, **help / helping** us to understand more about conservation issues.

Generally speaking, the program was a success. Most students improved their knowledge of wildlife conservation. **Moreover, / Therefore,** I would recommend this program to anyone who would like a good background in this field in a short time.

B Rewrite these extracts from a report using the expressions in parentheses. Sometimes you need to rewrite two sentences as one.

1. Our summer course was incredibly useful. I strongly recommend that you sign up for it. (therefore)

   _____

2. The teachers always prepared their lessons carefully. We never wasted any class time. (as a result)

   _____

3. Sometimes the guides were in a hurry to finish their talks. It was hard to follow them. (such . . . that)

   _____

4. The wildlife cruise was led by a brilliant naturalist. It was very informative. (consequently)

   _____

5. Some of the lectures were too technical. They demotivated some students. (so . . . that)

   _____

C Editing **Correct the mistakes. Sometimes there is more than one mistake and more than one correct answer. One sentence is correct.**

1. The summer course was excellent therefore I'm planning to major in wildlife management.
2. The ocean mammals course was such difficult some students lost interest.
3. The classes finished late, give us no time to relax before the field trips.
4. I had never seen a whale before therefore I was excited to go on the wildlife cruise.
5. One problem was that we had no free days, leaving us all exhausted by the end of the week.
6. Our group project was so success so we got the highest grade in the class.

D Write an evaluation of your favorite teacher. Explain why you like him or her.

Listening extra Resisting social pressures

A **Match the words and definitions. Write the letters a–e.**

1. to pursue a goal _____
2. a convention _____
3. to defy _____
4. an obstacle _____
5. to conform _____

a. to resist; to refuse to obey
b. something that's in the way
c. to obey; to follow rules
d. to try to achieve an aim
e. a rule or custom

B **Listen to an extract from a TV show. Are the sentences true or false? Write T or F.**

1. The talk show host thinks the topic of social pressure relates to everyone's life. _____
2. Susan has written several books about the psychology of social pressure. _____
3. Dr. Jones would like to settle into a more traditional life. _____
4. Jason was the first person in his family not to join the family business. _____
5. Susan thinks if people have a strong sense of personal identity, they can pursue their goals. _____
6. Jason was interested in a career in fashion, but still decided to become an artist. _____
7. Dr. Jones used to enjoy the same TV shows as other kids did. _____
8. Jason's family always understood that he wanted to choose art over business. _____

C **Listen again. Circle the correct option to complete each sentence.**

1. Susan **is / is not** the only person on the show who knows something about social pressure.
2. Dr. Jones works for **a hospital / several organizations**.
3. Dr. Jones is **single / married**.
4. As a child, Jason **did / did not** have a strong sense of his identity.
5. Growing up, Dr. Jones loved to watch **cartoons / documentaries** on TV.
6. Susan says that resisting social conventions is **difficult / natural**.

D **Answer the questions with your own ideas and opinions.**

About you

1. Why do you think most people conform to social norms?

_____

_____

2. Do you think that you are the kind of person who can resist social pressure? Why or why not?

_____

_____

3. Do you think that your society should allow people more freedom to make their own decisions about careers and family?

_____

_____

Now complete the *Unit 3 Progress chart* on page 98. Unit 3: Society **25**

Amazing world

Lesson A Vocabulary Animal behavior

A Match the words in bold with the words that have a similar meaning. Some sentences have two answers. Write the letters a–g.

| a. breed | b. burrows | c. colonies | d. feed | e. nest | f. predators | g. young |

1. The European rabbit lives in **large groups** in Spain, Portugal, and parts of Africa. _____
2. These rabbits live in networks of **holes**, which are also known as warrens. _____
3. Typically, these rabbits **eat** at night to avoid being attacked by **animals that kill and eat others**. _____ , _____
4. European rabbits can begin to **reproduce** when they are just four months old. _____
5. During pregnancy, female rabbits make a **comfortable and safe home**, where they can give birth to their **babies**. _____ , _____

B Complete the poster with the words in the box. Use each word only once.

| feed | hatch | hibernate | lay | mate | predators |

HELP SAVE THE MONARCH BUTTERFLIES!

Did you know that millions of monarch butterflies die each year because of human activity? Did you know that the milkweed plant, which is essential to the butterflies' survival, is being destroyed at an alarming rate?

Interesting facts about monarch butterflies

Monarch butterflies fly south from North America before the winter begins. During the winter months, the butterflies _____[1] in Mexico, where the climate is mild. In February and March, the butterflies start to _____[2] in order to reproduce. The butterflies _____[3] their eggs on milkweed plants. When the larvae _____[4], the caterpillars _____[5] on this same plant. In addition to providing food, the milkweed plant also gives the monarch butterflies poisonous chemicals that help them develop a defense against _____[6], such as frogs, birds, mice, and lizards.

Join the discussion on our online forum and help save these remarkable creatures.

About you

C Answer the questions with your own opinions.

1. Write about an animal or insect. Say why you find it interesting.

   _____

   _____

2. What do you think is the most interesting aspect of insect, bird, and animal migration?

   _____

   _____

Lesson A Grammar Talking about the past in the future

A **Circle the correct verb forms to complete the excerpt from a documentary. Sometimes both forms are possible.**

Biologists have made many fascinating discoveries about black bear hibernation. For example, prior to hibernating later this year, this black bear **will have gained / will have been gaining** at least 30 pounds every week over a period of several months. By the time she is in hibernation next year, her heartbeat **will have dropped / will have been dropping** to just eight beats per minute from around 40 to 50. In addition, her body temperature **will have decreased / will have been decreasing** by 12 degrees Fahrenheit. By spring, she **will have hibernated / will have been hibernating** for six months, and **will have lost / will have been losing** about 30 percent of her body weight.

B **Complete the sentences with the future perfect or future perfect continuous of the underlined verbs. Sometimes both forms are possible.**

1. Around November, this pregnant polar bear will enter her nest, or den, to give birth and <u>rest</u>.
   In January, she ___will have been resting___ for two months.
2. These Siberian marmots <u>hibernate</u> for eight months – from October to May.
   By March, they _____ for five months.
3. A shark <u>loses</u> approximately 1,800 teeth per year.
   At the end of the year, it _____ approximately 1,800 teeth.
4. An anteater <u>eats</u> 210,000 ants per week.
   In two weeks, this anteater _____ 420,000 ants.
5. The average female vampire bat can <u>consume</u> 20 grams (1 fluid ounce) of blood in 20 minutes.
   After 10 minutes, she _____ 10 grams (.5 fluid ounces) of blood.
6. A blue whale calf <u>gains</u> about 90 kilograms (200 pounds) every 24 hours.
   In 48 hours, a blue whale calf _____ about 180 kilograms (400 pounds).

About you

C **Answer the questions with your own views. Use the future perfect or future perfect continuous in your answers.**

1. How do you think the natural world will have changed in 50 years?

   _____

   _____

   _____

   _____

2. Do you think that conservation efforts will have benefitted any species that are endangered in 50 years time?

   _____

   _____

   _____

   _____

Lesson B Grammar Combining ideas

A Use the prepositional expressions in the box to replace the underlined parts of the sentences. Write the letters a–f. Some have more than one correct answer.

a. apart from	c. in addition to	e. due to the fact
b. as a result of	d. in line with	f. thanks to

1. <u>Because of</u> their amazing survival skills, scorpions are able to live in some of the harshest environments. _____
2. <u>According to</u> biologists' criteria for the classification of snakes, there are approximately 13,000 venomous species. _____
3. <u>Besides</u> offering protection from predators, quills help porcupines stay camouflaged. _____
4. <u>As well as</u> being able to run up to 42 kilometers (26 miles) per hour, roadrunners can also fly. _____
5. Peregrine falcons have become an endangered species <u>because of</u> the effects of pesticides in their bodies and eggshells. _____
6. Since the 1800s, the prairie dog population has decreased <u>for the reason</u> that humans have destroyed their habitats to build towns and villages. _____

B Circle the best prepositional expressions to complete the information.

By virtue of / In addition to its reputation as a symbol of the desert, the Saguaro cactus attracts a lot of attention. **Apart from / Thanks to** their ability to conserve water, Saguaro cacti can survive in even the driest environments. **On account of / In line with** their protective spines and slow growth, some of these plants can live for up to 150 years. **Apart from / In spite of** the fact that these cacti are very strong, cold weather and frost can kill them. Saguaro cacti produce white and yellow flowers **as a result of / in addition to** generating red fruit, which contain as many as 2,000 seeds. **Apart from / Due to** having one deep root that extends about two feet underground, Saguaro cacti have many smaller roots that are only four to six inches long. However, **as a result of / far from** its slow development and breeding, the cactus has become a candidate for the endangered species list. Many of these cacti are being illegally transplanted, sold, and placed in residential gardens, **far from / due to** the fact that they are rare and exotic.

Lesson C Conversation strategies

A Complete the expressions using the words in the box.

also	event	in	mention	top

Prof. Taylor   What do you think are the most urgent environmental problems?

Mario   Well, global warming, but _____[1] it seems like water is another issue, especially since a third of the world's population doesn't have access to clean water.

Jennifer   Yeah, I agree that water is major problem. On _____[2] of that, many of our fresh water sources are being polluted.

Fatima   Not to _____[3] the amount of water used for agricultural purposes.

Will   _____[4] any _____[5], we should manage water supplies better.

B Complete the conversation. Write the letters a–e.

> a. Not to mention the fact that fish is a major food source for billions of people.
> b. And also it's pretty bad that we allowed all that trash to collect in the first place.
> c. And what's more, they've even found hazardous waste.
> d. In any event, it's really bad for marine life.
> e. And on top of that, dolphins die because they get tangled up in trash.

Anthony   Did you watch that show about the Great Pacific Garbage Patch?

Sara   Yeah, I did. It was really disturbing.

Felipe   I didn't see it. What is it?

Anthony   Well, there's this huge trash dump floating in the middle of the Pacific. _____[1] I mean, can you imagine? Hazardous waste in the ocean?

Felipe   So does that toxic stuff end up in the fish we eat?

Sara   I guess. _____[2] You know, they drown.

Anthony   Yeah. _____[3]

Sara   Well, they'll have to do something about it to keep the oceans clean. _____[4]

Felipe   Yeah, people depend on it. So, is anyone doing anything to clean it all up?

Sara   Unfortunately not. It's seems like it's a complicated problem.

Anthony   Well, if you ask me, it's appalling. _____[5]

C Circle the best expressions to complete the conversation.

A   I was just reading this article about how the Siberian tiger is on the endangered species list.

B   Really? I didn't think that tigers had any predators.

A   Well, they don't – except humans. The biggest problems that affect them are pollution and deforestation. But **in any case, / and then** there *are* a lot of people who hunt them.

B   Huh. I guess people still enjoy the challenge of hunting them. **In addition, / Not to mention** the fact that their fur is pretty valuable.

A   Yeah. **And then / In any event**, they're hunted for body parts, too. **Also / In any case**, I think we should join an environmental group. Maybe we can do something.

Lesson D Reading Animals and earthquakes

A Prepare How do you think some animals detect an earthquake? What unusual behaviors do they display before an earthquake? Check (✔) the boxes.

Detection
☐ They feel the temperature drop.
☐ They detect the earth moving.
☐ They notice changes in chemistry.

Behavior
☐ They remain in water.
☐ They leave their mating sites.
☐ They become magnetic.

B Read the article. Check your guesses from Exercise A.

Toads able to detect earthquake days beforehand, study says

1 Toads may be able to detect earthquakes days before they hit, according to a study which reveals how the creatures deserted their mating site before Italy's L'Aquila quake last year. Toads may be able to detect imminent earthquakes, according to scientists. The finding will add to the accounts through the centuries where animals, from dogs to rats, snakes, and chickens, are said to have behaved strangely before an earthquake.

2 In the study published today in the *Journal of Zoology*, a colony of toads deserted their mating site three days before an earthquake struck in L'Aquila — the epicenter was 74 kilometers from the area where the animals had normally gathered. No toads returned to the site until 10 days later, after the last of the significant aftershocks had finished.

3 The discovery was made by accident by Rachel Grant, a life scientist at the Open University. She was studying the effects of lunar cycles on the toads' behavior and reproduction. "I was going out every evening at dusk and counting how many toads were active and how many pairs there were. Normally they arrive for breeding in early March and you get large numbers of males at the breeding site. The females get paired fairly quickly. They stay active and obvious around the breeding site until the spawning is over in April or May."

4 One day she noticed there were no toads. "Sometimes during the breeding season you get a drop in numbers if there's been a very cold night, but usually the day after, they come back again. It was very unusual that there was none at all."

5 There could be several mechanisms for animals to sense the beginnings of an earthquake, wrote Grant in the *Journal of Zoology*. They could detect seismic waves directly or ground tilt (which can occur in the minutes before a quake). In addition, there might be anomalies in the earth's magnetic field.

6 Looking for clues to explain the toads' behavior, Grant found that scientists had noticed disruptions in the ionosphere, the uppermost electromagnetic layer of the earth's atmosphere, at the time of the L'Aquila earthquake, which the toads may have detected. Previous earthquakes have had similar ionospheric disruptions associated with them. "I've spoken to seismologists who said there were a lot of gases released before the earthquake, a lot of charged particles. Toads and amphibians are very sensitive to changes in environmental chemistry, and I think these gases and charged particles could have been detected by the toads."

7 Previously, fish, rodents, and snakes have been anecdotally associated with unusual behavior more than a week before an earthquake or at distances greater than 50 kilometers.

8 In 2003, Japanese doctor Kiyoshi Shimamura said that there was a jump in dog bites and other dog-related complaints before and after earthquakes. Before the 1995 earthquake in Kobe, a disaster that killed more than 6,000 people, he found that accounts of dogs barking "excessively" went up by 18 percent on average in the months before the earthquake. Above the epicenter on Awaji Island, there was a 60 percent increase in complaints compared with a year earlier.

9 Grant's work is not the first time toads have been associated with sensing the precursors of earthquakes. "In 2008, there was a big earthquake in Szechuan province in China, and there was unusual migration of toads seen," she said. "I'd like to study it further and look at animal behavior in combination with seismological and geophysical precursors."

SOURCE: *The Guardian*

C Paraphrase Find the paragraph that each the sentence summarizes.

1. Toads might have felt the variations in gases in the earth's atmosphere. _____
2. There have been many stories about the changes in fish, snake, and rodent behavior before an earthquake or natural disaster. _____
3. Recent research shows that toads might be able to predict earthquakes. _____
4. Grant noticed the toads' change in behavior while conducting an unrelated study. _____
5. Others have noticed the change in toads' behavior before an earthquake. _____
6. Toads left their mating site before the L'Aquila earthquake. _____

D Check your understanding Answer the questions. Check (✔) a, b, or c.

1. How did scientists discover that toads might be able to detect earthquakes?
   a. They started hibernating early.
   b. They left the places where they normally breed.
   c. They stopped breeding for several months.
2. What was Rachel Grant studying when she made her discovery?
   a. the migration pattern of toads
   b. the impact of earthquakes on the toads' behavior
   c. the effect of the moon on the toads' mating behavior
3. What does Grant think affected the toads before the earthquake?
   a. a change in temperature
   b. a change in the weather patterns
   c. a change in the environmental chemistry
4. What was one of Kiyoshi Shimamura's discoveries about the Kobe earthquake?
   a. Reports of dog barking increased by 18 percent.
   b. Toads left their mating site.
   c. The number of dog bites decreased by 60 percent.

E Read for detail Are the sentences true or false, or is the information not given in the article? Write T, F, or NG. Correct the false sentences.

1. Two days before an earthquake struck in L'Aquila, toads left their mating sites. _____
2. Toads are nocturnal and mate at night. _____
3. Animals might be able to feel seismic waves. _____
4. Grant thinks that toads can sense a change in the gases released before an earthquake. _____
5. Before every earthquake in Japan, dog barking has increased. _____
6. In the 2008 earthquake in China, toads followed their usual migration patterns. _____

About you

F React Answer the questions with your own opinions.

1. What was the most interesting aspect of the article?

   _____

   _____

2. What did you learn from the article?

   _____

   _____

Writing A persuasive essay

A Read the introduction to a persuasive essay. What is the author's argument? What evidence does the author present as support? Then circle the correct prepositions.

Can animals predict natural disasters?

The belief that animals can predict earthquakes has existed for centuries **throughout / in terms of** Asia, but was largely based **beneath / upon** anecdotal evidence. Until fairly recently, the idea was dismissed **within / upon** the scientific community. However, research has shown that some species may well be able to sense changes in the earth's environment **amongst / within** a short time of a natural disaster occurring. Studies have revealed that **prior to / beneath** an earthquake, toads alter their breeding and migration habits, and dogs tend to bark more. Likewise, fish exhibit signs of panic when exposed to electromagnetic pulses similar to those of an earthquake. Taken together, the behavioral changes of toads, fish, and dogs appear to confirm the belief **amongst / in terms of** many ancient cultures that animals are sensitive to environmental changes caused by natural disasters and therefore can be said to predict them.

B Complete the paragraph with the expressions in the box.

amongst	beneath	in terms of	throughout	upon	within

Studying the behavior of animals can save lives. _____[1] history, people have depended _____[2] animals to predict natural disasters. One example is the 1975 earthquake in Haicheng, China. Biologists guessed that snakes and earthworms must have detected electromagnetic changes _____[3] the earth's surface because they suddenly left their warm burrows in the middle of winter. The biologists then alerted the authorities of a possible earthquake, and _____[4] 24 hours the city was evacuated. After the magnitude 7.3 earthquake struck, officials realized that with all the destruction, many people might have been killed. _____[5] scientists, the credibility of this story has been debated. However, one can clearly see that _____[6] saving lives, such a prediction was highly valuable for the residents of Haicheng.

C Editing Correct the mistakes in these sentences. One sentence is correct.

1. Many scientists disagree the idea that animals can predict earthquakes.
2. Scientists are now looking upon changes in animal behavior before natural disasters in greater detail.
3. Scientists cannot rely anecdotal evidence to prove their point.
4. If you look upon the facts, it seems certain that the climate is changing.
5. In the future, humans might depend our pets to predict natural disasters.
6. Some scientists look upon ancient beliefs about animals as superstition.

D Write a persuasive essay to answer the question: *Are animals smarter than humans think?* State your opinion and support your ideas with evidence.

Listening extra Remarkable raccoons

A **Look at the photos. What do you know about raccoons? Check (✔) the adjectives you would use to describe these raccoons.**

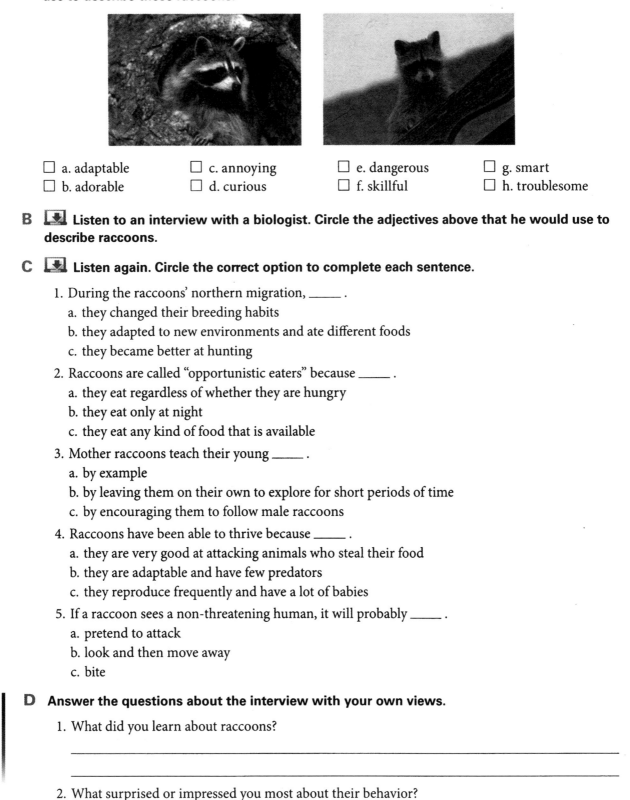

☐ a. adaptable   ☐ c. annoying   ☐ e. dangerous   ☐ g. smart

☐ b. adorable   ☐ d. curious   ☐ f. skillful   ☐ h. troublesome

B 🔽 **Listen to an interview with a biologist. Circle the adjectives above that he would use to describe raccoons.**

C 🔽 **Listen again. Circle the correct option to complete each sentence.**

1. During the raccoons' northern migration, _____ .
   a. they changed their breeding habits
   b. they adapted to new environments and ate different foods
   c. they became better at hunting

2. Raccoons are called "opportunistic eaters" because _____ .
   a. they eat regardless of whether they are hungry
   b. they eat only at night
   c. they eat any kind of food that is available

3. Mother raccoons teach their young _____ .
   a. by example
   b. by leaving them on their own to explore for short periods of time
   c. by encouraging them to follow male raccoons

4. Raccoons have been able to thrive because _____ .
   a. they are very good at attacking animals who steal their food
   b. they are adaptable and have few predators
   c. they reproduce frequently and have a lot of babies

5. If a raccoon sees a non-threatening human, it will probably _____ .
   a. pretend to attack
   b. look and then move away
   c. bite

About you

D **Answer the questions about the interview with your own views.**

1. What did you learn about raccoons?

_____

_____

2. What surprised or impressed you most about their behavior?

_____

_____

Now complete the *Unit 4 Progress chart* on page 99.

Lesson A Vocabulary Gadgets

A **Complete the sentences with the words in the box.**

| compact | functional | innovative | integral | obsolete | portable |

1. Being aware of what people want from their phones and devices is a/an _____ part of our marketing strategy. It's central to what we do.
2. It is also important to come up with our own new ideas and be _____ .
3. Of course our products need to be _____ and do what people want them to do, but attractive design is also important nowadays.
4. Most people want devices that are easy to carry – in other words, _____ .
5. They also want phones that are _____ enough to fit into a purse or pocket.
6. As technology changes faster and faster, many of this year's products will become _____ in two years' time.

B **Complete the article with the words in the box. Sometimes more than one answer is possible.**

| countless | humble | rudimentary | significant | standard |

A short history of cell phones

It seems difficult to imagine life without cell phones these days. Over time, they have become a _____[1] accessory, which most of us never leave home without. They have affected our ability to communicate and interact with the world in _____[2] ways.

The development of the technology in the U.S. started in the 1940s, and the first mobile phone call was made from an automobile in 1946. Martin Cooper, who worked for Motorola, is credited with making the first call from a handheld phone in 1973. The design of that phone seems _____[3] now. It weighed 1.13 kilos (2.5 pounds) and was 22.8 centimeters (9 inches) long!

Since those _____[4] beginnings, there have been _____[5] developments in both technology and design. The result is that phones today are viewed as a convenience that most of us would not want to live without.

About you **C** **Answer the questions with your own ideas.**

1. What was the last gadget you bought? How has it changed your life?

_____

_____

2. What do you feel is the most innovative or significant device from the last decade? Why?

_____

_____

Lesson A Grammar Information focus 1

A Read the article. Write the adverb in parentheses in the correct place. Sometimes more than one answer is possible.

Who wouldn't want a personal jetpack? Ever since James Bond was seen launching off in the 1965 movie *Thunderball*, the personal jetpack has _____ — been ___*eagerly*___ [1] anticipated (eagerly) as an alternative form of transportation. We are still waiting. However, innovative gadgets are _____ being _____ [2] invented (continually) in the fields of transportation, energy, and communication – at even faster rates than ever before.

The amount of money that has _____ been _____ [3] injected (reportedly) into the development of new technology in the last decade is unprecedented. Every major corporation – and every new company – wants to be the first to come out with the next bestselling idea. With the kind of money that is _____ being _____ [4] invested (heavily) in these fields, there will definitely be more ground-breaking innovation – even if we do not know what it is yet. This is especially true because most of the research and development of new technologies has _____ been _____ [5] done (apparently) under a shield of secrecy.

And, what about that personal jetpack? I would bet that development is _____ being _____ [6] worked on (still) somewhere. I plan to be one of the first in line when it finally comes onto the market!

B Rewrite the sentences. Rewrite the underlined clauses in the passive and add the adverbs given. Sometimes there is more than one correct word order.

1. <u>They were developing hybrid cars</u> (intensively) long before they were on the market.

   _____

2. In fact, <u>they have made hybrid cars</u> (apparently) since the beginning of the auto industry.

   _____

3. <u>Someone had built a hybrid car</u> (already) in 1899.

   _____

4. <u>They had presented that hybrid car</u> (originally) at the 1900 World Fair in Paris.

   _____

5. It was a long time before <u>they were mass producing hybrid cars</u> (finally) in the 1990s.

   _____

6. It seems incredible, but by the end of 1997 <u>they had sold only 300 hybrid cars</u>. (reportedly)

   _____

7. Today, <u>they are improving the designs</u>, (continually) and <u>people are driving hybrid cars</u>. (increasingly) _____

About you

C Answer the questions with your own ideas.

1. What changes do you imagine are currently being worked on for the next generation of cars?

   _____

2. Which of the gadgets that you use have been significantly improved over recent years?

   _____

Lesson B Grammar Information focus 2

A Rewrite the underlined parts of the article using the passive forms of past modal verbs.

In May 2010, Jessica Watson completed a round-the-world solo voyage, arriving in Sydney Harbour just three days before her seventeenth birthday. Her journey was not without danger or controversy.

Certainly, Jessica sailed through some dangerous waters and, indeed, something could easily have killed her. _she could easily have been killed._ [1] The list of risks was long. Pirates could have attacked her. _____ [2] Larger vessels could have also hit her sailboat _____ [3] – indeed such an incident occurred prior to her voyage. Bad weather was a constant danger and heavy seas might well have damaged or destroyed her boat. _____ [4] And, in a worst case scenario, she could have fallen overboard and sharks might have attacked her. _____ [5]

Despite the risks, Jessica survived, but there was a lot of controversy around her trip because of her age. Many people felt that her parents should not have allowed such a young person _____ [6] to undertake a dangerous trip. People say they ought not to have permitted it _____. [7]

B Rewrite the sentences in the passive.

1. They should have made her parents stop her.
   Her parents should have been made to stop her.

2. They might have made her call the authorities every day.
   _____

3. They shouldn't have made her parents feel guilty.
   _____

4. They could have made her go with an older person.
   _____

5. They should have made her gain more experience before her first solo trip.
   _____

6. They could have made her wait until she was older to take the trip.
   _____

About you

C Answer the questions with your own ideas and opinions.

1. Think of a recent achievement by someone in the news. What are some things that might have happened to bring about a different result?
   _____
   _____

2. What was one thing that you were made to do when you were a child that you now realize helped you to become who you are today?
   _____
   _____

Lesson C Conversation strategies

A Circle the correct expressions to complete the conversation.

Clara I think it's always fascinating to read about the research that's going on. I mean, **just think about it / to put it another way**. It just seems like everything scientists do leads to some breakthrough.

Emma Well, **definitely / not necessarily**. I mean, **look at it this way: / let me put it another way:** they've spent billions trying to cure the common cold. I mean, yes, you can take medicine, but it doesn't cure your cold or stop you from getting one. **To put it another way, / Just think,** research doesn't always lead to something useful.

Clara **Maybe not / Just think**. But it's still worth doing. I mean, **just think about it / one way to look at it is** that you don't really know if you're going to make progress until you actually do the research. That's just the way it is.

Emma Yeah. I guess there is no way to know.

B Match the sentences and responses. Write the letters a–e. There is one extra response.

1. Do you think world peace is possible? _____
2. Don't you think a lot of money has been completely wasted on unnecessary medical research in recent years? _____
3. I think more research effort should be put into studying the oceans. We could learn a lot from that. _____
4. It seems like so much money has been put into space exploration and most of it's been wasted.

   _____

a. Absolutely. They haven't really been fully explored and you never know what might be discovered there.
b. Maybe, but there's already been a lot of research on animals.
c. Probably not. There'll always be something people are fighting about.
d. Not necessarily. There have been countless discoveries that have come from it, either directly or indirectly. Think of satellite technology, for example. I think it's been valuable.
e. Definitely not. I think any research is worth it. You never know what treatments or cures might be discovered.

C Complete the conversation with the expressions in the box. Some may have more than one correct answer.

Absolutely	Let me put it another way	Look at it this way	Maybe	✓ Not necessarily

Stephan I think scientists spend more and more money on research that seems so useless.

Andrea <u>Not necessarily</u>[1]. It may seem useless, but you never know what they might discover. _____[2]. There are quite a few scientific discoveries that happened purely by chance. For example, those sticky notes that we all use . . . they're really convenient, aren't they?

Stephan _____[3]. I use them all the time.

Andrea Well, the inventor was trying to make a strong glue, and he thought he'd failed. But, it turns out that he'd created something useful. So it wasn't a waste of time.

Stephan _____[4]. I don't know. . . . That's not saving lives though, is it?

Andrea _____[5]. Penicillin saves lives, and that was discovered by accident.

Lesson D Reading Pen and paper

A Prepare What did people write on before the invention of paper? Make a list. Then scan the article to see how many of your ideas are included.

B Read for topic Read the article. What was the main challenge in the development of a writing surface?

    a. making it inexpensive

    b. developing something easy to make and carry

    c. finding a writing instrument to use on the surface

THE INVENTION OF PAPER

1 Written communication has been the center of civilization for centuries. Most of our important records are on paper. Although writing has been around for a long time, paper hasn't.

2 In fact, putting thoughts down in written form wasn't always easy or practical. Early people discovered that they could make simple drawings on the walls of caves, which was a great place for recording thoughts, but wasn't portable.

3 Imagine spending hours scratching a message into a heavy clay tablet and then having to transport it. That's exactly what the Sumerians did around 4000 BCE. Although this form of written communication was now portable, it still wasn't practical because of its weight.

4 For centuries, people tried to discover better surfaces on which to record their thoughts. Almost everything imaginable was tried. Wood, stone, ceramics, cloth, bark, metal, silk, bamboo, and tree leaves were all used as a writing surface at one time or another.

5 The word *paper* is derived from the word *papyrus,* which was a plant found in Egypt along the lower Nile River. About 5,000 years ago, Egyptians created "sheets" of papyrus by harvesting, peeling, and slicing the plant into strips. The strips were then layered, pounded together, and smoothed to make a flat, uniform sheet.

6 No major changes in writing materials were to come for about 3,000 years. The person credited with inventing paper is a Chinese man named Ts'ai Lun. He took the inner bark of a mulberry tree and bamboo fibers, mixed them with water, and pounded them with a wooden tool. He then poured this mixture onto a flat piece of coarsely woven cloth and let the water drain through, leaving only the fibers on the cloth. Once dry, Ts'ai Lun discovered that he had created a quality writing surface that was relatively easy to make and was lightweight. This knowledge of papermaking was used in China before word was passed along to Korea, Samarkand, Baghdad, and Damascus.

7 By the tenth century, Arabians were substituting linen fibers for wood and bamboo, creating a finer sheet of paper. Although paper was of fairly high quality now, the only way to reproduce written work was by hand, a painstaking process.

8 By the twelfth century, papermaking reached Europe. In 1448, Johannes Gutenberg, a German, was credited with inventing the printing press. (It is believed that moveable type was actually invented hundreds of years earlier in Asia.) Books and other important documents could now be reproduced quickly. This method of printing in large quantities led to a rapid increase in the demand for paper.

SOURCE: Wisconsin Paper Council

C Information flow **Put the following important events in the development of paper into chronological order.**

_____ a. Papermaking occurred in China.

_____ b. Arabians substituted linen fibers for wood.

_____ c. Clay tablets are used by the Sumerians.

_____ d. The printing press is invented in Germany.

_____ e. Egyptians created sheets of papyrus.

_____ f. People discovered cave walls were a good place for drawings.

D Read for detail **Are the sentences true or false, or is the information not given in the article? Write T, F, or NG. Correct the false sentences.**

1. Cave paintings drawn by early people have been found all over the world. _____

2. Sumerians used clay tablets for writing around 3000 BCE. _____

3. At one time, tree leaves and tree bark were tried as a surface for writing. _____

4. Papyrus is found near water in Egypt. _____

5. There are three steps in the process of making paper from papyrus. _____

6. Egyptians used plants to make a kind of ink for writing on papyrus. _____

7. An Egyptian man is credited with inventing the first real paper. _____

8. Ts'ai Lun used plant fibers only in the process of making paper. _____

9. Ts'ai Lun worked on his process for making paper for many years before he was successful. _____

10. People were making paper in Korea, Samarkand, Baghdad, and Damascus at the same time as Ts'ai Lun in China. _____

11. The paper made by Arabians was better quality than previous paper. _____

12. Johannes Gutenberg invented moveable type and the printing press. _____

13. The invention of the printing press led to an increase in demand for paper. _____

14. Important documents are frequently kept in a digital or 'paperless' format. _____

About you

E React **Answer the questions with your own ideas and opinions.**

1. Which stage in the development of paper do you think was most important? Why?

_____

_____

2. How do you think the invention of the printing press changed the course of human development and history?

_____

_____

3. What do you think is the future of paper? Do you think paper will become obsolete?

_____

_____

Writing An opinion essay

A **Read the introduction to an opinion essay. Which statement would the writer agree with — a, b, or c?**

    a. Schools should only teach keyboarding skills.
    b. Schools should only teach handwriting.
    c. Schools should teach both keyboarding and handwriting.

Writing by hand vs. writing digitally: Same or different?

    It has been suggested that the art of writing with a pen or pencil is not worth teaching anymore. It is generally recognized that young people are already more comfortable working on a computer or tablet screen than on paper. Certainly, the skill of good handwriting is no longer as respected as it used to be. It often seems the only reason to learn how to write in cursive these days is to write signatures. However, there are those who disagree that there is no value in teaching handwriting anymore. For example, some say that writing digitally does not involve the same thought process as writing with a pen or pencil. They question whether writing digitally affects creativity differently than handwriting. I agree that writing digitally and writing by hand are likely very different processes. However, I would argue that completely replacing handwriting with keyboarding could lead to a loss, whether a loss in creativity or a loss that we have not even realized yet.

B **Rewrite the sentences using _it_ clauses in the passive.**

    1. People generally accept that there will be less need for paper in the future.
       It is generally accepted that there will be less need for paper in the future.

    2. People widely recognize that fewer people are printing documents because they can store them electronically.

       _____

    3. People often suggest that there are many aspects of our current lives that will not be preserved for the future because of the absence of paper documents, such as personal letters.

       _____

    4. People have also suggested that the reading process on a screen may differ from the process of reading a printed book.

       _____

    5. People generally recognize that digital storage is an environmentally friendly option.

       _____

C Editing **Correct the mistakes. There is one error in each sentence.**

    1. Do you believe that writing on a screen, rather than paper, effects creativity in any way?
    2. Nevertheless writing on a computer might be faster than writing by hand, many wonder whether writing skills are being lost in the process.
    3. Researchers are not yet sure whether the affects of new technology are positive or negative for students.
    4. In the one hand, writing on a computer or tablet is faster. On the one hand, it doesn't work if there is a power outage and your battery runs out.

D **Write an opinion essay to answer the question: _Should elementary schools stop teaching students how to write in cursive and use the time for other subjects?_ Support your opinion with reasons and examples.**

Listening extra New apps

A Look at the photo. Which of these apps are you familiar with? What other apps do you use? How often do you use them? Complete the chart.

Use multiple times a day:	
Use once or twice a day:	
Use a few times a week:	
Use occasionally:	
Never use:	

B 🔽 Listen to the conversation. Circle the correct option to complete each sentence.

1. Pieter shows Aisha a music app that
   a. they both want.   b. they both have.   c. Aisha doesn't know about.

2. Pieter mentions
   a. one idea for an app.   b. two ideas for apps.   c. no ideas for apps.

3. Aisha mentions
   a. one idea for an app.   b. two ideas for apps.   c. no ideas for apps.

4. Their app ideas are
   a. all practical and functional.   b. all for amusement and fun.   c. both practical and fun.

C 🔽 Listen again. Are the sentences true or false? Write T or F.

1. Pieter's app would only be helpful to find ATMs. _____
2. The name of Pieter's app is "Where's the nearest . . . ?" _____
3. Aisha thinks Pieter's app idea is original and new. _____
4. Aisha has two ideas for apps, and both are very amusing ideas. _____
5. One of Aisha's apps would help people keep track of money they save. _____
6. Pieter thinks ease of use would be important for this app. _____
7. Aisha's other app would use cartoon characters. _____
8. Aisha knows which cartoon character she would like to be. _____

About you

D Answer the questions.

1. Do you use any of the apps mentioned? Would you like to? Why or why not?

   _____

2. What new app would you like to see? What would it do?

   _____

Now complete the *Unit 5 Progress chart* on page 99.   Unit 5: Progress   **41**

Business studies

Lesson A Grammar Adding and modifying information

A Read the article on advertising. Complete the relative clauses.

ADVERTISING: Can it become counterproductive?

Research shows that the popularity of a product depends greatly on the amount and extent of advertising. Repeated exposure to ads can produce positive feelings in potential customers, some _of whom_ [1] will become consumers of the product.

Moreover, successful advertising campaigns, some _____ [2] continue for 10 years or more, can ensure that a brand name will become firmly fixed in people's minds. Research also shows, however, that there is a tipping point at _____ [3] an ad campaign can become counterproductive. This happens when the customers to _____ [4] the product is targeted become overexposed, causing their positive feelings to become negative. It's not clear, however, how this research applies to Internet pop-up ads, most _____ [5] are universally disliked, as they often cover up material people are trying to read. Pop-up ads would appear to be counterproductive, as they rarely produce positive feelings in Internet users, almost all _____ [6] find them extremely intrusive. Nevertheless, some research shows that pop-up ads are actually very successful, and the prediction is that people will soon find them just as acceptable as other forms of advertising.

B Read the comments posted by readers of the article. Rewrite each first sentence using a relative clause with a pronoun or a preposition after the underlined word.

Laidback: Pop-up ads are an interesting <u>topic</u>, and I'm only too familiar with this topic, unfortunately. They're so annoying.
1. _Pop-up ads are an interesting topic, with which I'm only too familiar, unfortunately._

MadBrad: Every day I struggle with <u>pop-up ads</u>, and some of them can't be closed with a simple click. A click just takes you to their website!
2. _____

CoolHead: I don't pay much attention to <u>pop-up ads</u> as most of them advertise products I'm not interested in anyway. I ignore them.
3. _____

Maggie95: Absolutely – I can tell you that none of my <u>friends</u> can stand pop-up ads and most of them spend long hours on the Internet.
4. _____

Dino: Well, this is an interesting <u>phenomenon</u>, and a lot has been written about it. Negative feelings are often directed at the website, not the product.
5. _____

PennyPincher: Well, I subscribe to an Internet <u>service</u>, and I pay a lot of money for it every month. So why do I have to look at ads just to get into my email?
6. _____

BroadView: This is a difficult <u>problem</u>, and there seems to be no obvious solution to it. Advertising is here to stay.
7. _____

Kittie: Yes, websites are offering us a valuable <u>service</u>, and they have to pay for it with advertising. It's no different from television.
8. _____

Lesson B Vocabulary Attracting and deterring

A Read the list of dos and don'ts for people studying to get their realtors' license. Circle the best option to complete each piece of advice.

1. If you are trying to **woo / intimidate** new clients, listen to them carefully and refer often to what they have said in order to show you understand their needs and concerns.

2. Keep your car clean! Driving clients around in a messy or dirty car tends to **persuade them / put them off**, making it likely they will look for another realtor.

3. Don't show clients homes that are above their price range at the beginning. This can **scare them off / tempt them**. Instead, start out by showing them a property in their price range that won't **coax / appeal** to them.

4. Never **discourage / entice** clients by telling them a property is too expensive for them.

5. Never try to **pressure clients into / deter clients from** buying a property they don't really want because they won't be happy, and they won't recommend you to their friends.

6. The best way to **alienate / attract** new clients is through word of mouth. So treat all clients with care and respect so they will recommend you to their friends.

B Complete the conversation about renting an apartment with the correct forms of the verbs in the box. Sometimes there is more than one correct answer.

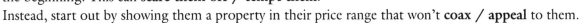

attract	convince	discourage	draw...in	lure	pressure...into	put...off

A I hear you're looking for an apartment.

B Yeah, well, I was hoping to live with my parents a bit longer, but they _____[1] me that it was time to find my own place, you know, now that I have a job.

A Have you seen any good possibilities?

B Not really. Actually, I'm not happy with my realtor. She's always trying to _____ me _____[2] renting places that I don't like. I get the feeling she doesn't listen to anything I say.

A I don't know why some realtors act like that. How do they expect to _____[3] new clients if they treat people that way? So how did you find this company?

B Well, they _____[4] me with this ad for a luxury apartment with low rent. But even though I called them immediately, the apartment was no longer available! They had other places to show me, but of course they were all more expensive.

A Oh, I know. It's a case of deceptive advertising. They do that to _____ new customers _____[5].

B Yeah, that's something that really _____ me _____[6]. But I've heard that all management companies do it.

A Well, don't let that _____[7] you. I'm sure you'll find something suitable.

About you

C Answer the questions with vocabulary from Exercises A and B where possible.

1. Have you ever been lured by a deceptive ad? What happened exactly?

_____

_____

2. Has a salesperson ever tried to pressure you into buying something? How did you feel about it?

_____

_____

Lesson B Grammar Referring to people and things

A Circle the correct words to complete the email to department store employees.

To: Sales staff   From: Management team   Date: November 20

Thanks to all of you for agreeing to work longer hours this Friday during our one-day pre-holiday sale. I want to go over some special instructions for one-day sales. **Any / Some** of you are already familiar with these, and **others / another** are not, but I'd like everyone to go over them carefully.

When the store opens at 6:00 a.m., customers will already be lined up outside. **Some / Any** will be impatient. Do not slow down traffic by standing in the main aisles.

Some / Another popular items will be "flying off the shelves." If you notice the stock of an item running low, call the stockroom to bring up more merchandise. This way, any potential conflict between customers can be avoided.

Customers may have to wait in line for our most popular sales items. **Any / Some** customer that tries to cut in line should be directed to the end of the line. **Any / Some** serious arguments that break out should be handled by security.

We will run out of the most popular merchandise before noon. Try to persuade disappointed customers to consider **other / another** similar items so that they still purchase something.

Any / Some salesperson working at the cash registers needs to be aware of how many people are waiting in line. If **some / any** line is longer than five people, you need to notify management so that **another / other** register can be opened right away.

I know **some / any** of you have complained in the past about the loud music we play all day. Please keep in mind that our research indicates that this type of music encourages people to buy.

Finally, as always, **some / any** customers will be polite and courteous and **other / others** customers will not. Remain calm and treat people with courtesy no matter how they act toward you.

Thank you again for your dedication and hard work!

B Complete the conversation between two salespeople with the words in the box.

another	any	some	some other	other	others

A Wow! What a day! I'm really exhausted! _____[1] of the customers were nice, but _____[2] were kind of rude.

B Actually, _____[3] were totally rude. I mean, one of my customers was reaching for a laptop he wanted when _____[4] customer came up and grabbed it. I had to call security.

A Well, one of my customers got into a fight with some _____[5] customers who saw him cutting in line for wide-screen TVs.

B Well, thank goodness for the security guards. It seemed like they were pretty tough on _____[6] customer who got into a fight.

A The music didn't help. _____[7] people liked it, but it was driving _____[8] crazy.

B You can say that again. We should suggest _____[9] kind of music for next year.

A I don't know. _____[10] suggestion I make to that new manager is ignored.

B Well, if the _____[11] one is working tomorrow, you know, the nice one, tell her.

About you

C Answer the questions with information that is true for you.

1. Do you like to shop in stores when there are big sales? Why or why not?

_____

2. What kinds of things have you bought on sale? Have you found any good bargains?

_____

Lesson C Conversation strategies

A Complete the conversation with the questions in the box.

But aren't things changing?	So, that's a good thing, isn't it?
Couldn't that be the reason for the gap?	So, shouldn't they earn just as much as men?
So, it really isn't fair, is it?	That's still a big gap, don't you think?

A You know, it's really annoying that women still don't earn as much as men.

B Yeah, but the wage gap has closed a lot over the last 50 years. Women earn more now than they ever did before. _____¹

A I guess it is, and things *are* better than they used to be, but women still only earn about 77 percent of what men earn. _____²

B Yeah, I guess that is still a significant difference. But more men finish college than women. _____³

A No, actually, I read that more women get college degrees than men. What's more, women with the very same education and working in the same jobs still earn less than men. _____⁴

B No, it's not, I agree. There's still some inequality. _____⁵
I just read that more women are becoming the primary wage earners in their families.

A Right. But think about it. Women now have more and more responsibility for supporting their families. _____⁶

B Rewrite the questions in the conversation in Exercise A. Change the tag questions to negative questions and change the negative questions to tag questions.

1. _____
2. _____
3. _____
4. _____
5. _____
6. _____

C Rewrite each of Speaker A's statements as a negative question and as a tag question. Add *granted* to the correct places in Speaker B's replies. Add commas where necessary.

1. *A* The government needs more money for infrastructure projects. So people need to pay higher taxes.
   Doesn't the government need more money for infrastructure projects?
   The government needs more money for infrastructure projects, doesn't it?

   B _____ the government needs more tax revenue, but _____ corporations also benefit from government projects, so they should pay higher taxes, too.

2. *A* Companies have a responsibility to ensure that they don't cause any environmental damage.
   _____
   _____

   B Well, _____ the government really needs to pass more legislation to protect the environment, but companies should take more responsibility, _____ .

3. *A* It's really unfair when a company doesn't have equal numbers of male and female managers.
   _____
   _____

   B Well, _____ it is unfair. But it can be difficult to fix that.

Lesson D Reading Natural disasters and businesses

A Prepare Write down three things that a business would want to protect in the event of a natural disaster. Then scan the article to see if your ideas are mentioned.

1. _____ 2. _____ 3. _____

B Read for main ideas Read the article. What important items should a business protect from a natural disaster?

Protect Business Records and Inventory

PROTECTING YOUR PROPERTY FROM NATURAL HAZARDS

1   Most businesses keep on-site records and files (both hardcopy and electronic) that are essential to normal operations. Some businesses also store raw materials and product inventory. The loss of essential records, files, and other materials during a disaster is commonplace and can not only add to your damage costs but also delay your return to normal operations. The longer your business is not operating, the more likely you are to lose customers permanently to your competitors.

2   To reduce your vulnerability, determine which records, files, and materials are most important; consider their vulnerability to damage during different types of disasters (such as floods, hurricanes, and earthquakes) and take steps to protect them, including the following:
- Raising computers above the flood level and moving them away from large windows
- Moving heavy and fragile objects to low shelves
- Storing vital documents (plans, legal papers, etc.) in a secure off-site location
- Regularly backing up vital electronic files (such as billing and payroll records and customer lists) and storing backup copies in a secure off-site location
- Securing equipment that could move or fall during an earthquake
- Prior to hurricanes, cover or protect vital documents and electrical equipment from potential wind driven rain, which may breech the building envelope through windows, doors, or roof systems.

TIPS

3   Keep these points in mind when protecting your business records and inventory:
- Make sure you are aware of the details of your flood insurance and other hazard insurance policies, specifically which items and contents are covered and under what conditions. For example, if you have a home business, you may need two flood insurance policies, a home policy and a separate business policy, depending on the percentage of the total square footage of your house that is devoted to business use. Check with your insurance agent if you have questions about any of your policies.
- When you identify equipment susceptible to damage, consider the location of the equipment. For example, equipment near a hot water tank or pipes could be damaged if the pipes burst during an earthquake, and equipment near large windows could be damaged during hurricanes.
- Assign disaster mitigation duties to your employees. For example, some employees could be responsible for securing storage bins and others for backing up computer files and delivering copies to a secure location.
- You may want to consider having other offices of your company or a contractor perform some administrative duties, such as maintaining payroll records or providing customer service.
- Estimate the cost of repairing or replacing each essential piece of equipment in your business. Your estimates will help you assess your vulnerability and focus your efforts.
- For both insurance and tax purposes, you should maintain written and photographic inventories of all important materials and equipment. The inventory should be stored in a safety deposit box or other secure location.
- Periodically evaluate the building envelope to make sure that wind and water are not able to penetrate the building. Do regular maintenance and repairs to maintain the strength of the building envelope.

SOURCE: U.S. Department of Homeland Security - FEMA

C Check your understanding **Check (✔) the correct answer to each question.**

1. The most serious consequence of not being prepared for a natural disaster is that . . .
   _____ a. your computer equipment may get damaged.
   _____ b. you may lose business.
   _____ c. you may lose your payroll records.
2. The suggestions are divided into two sections that outline . . .
   _____ a. things to do before an emergency and things to do after an emergency.
   _____ b. suggestions for business owners and suggestions for business employees.
   _____ c. how to protect the most important things and suggestions for other actions to take.
3. The article suggests that precautionary actions need to be taken . . .
   _____ a. once.
   _____ b. yearly.
   _____ c. regularly.

D Read for inference **Why do you think the article suggests these actions? Match each suggestion with a probable reason.**

1. Raise computers above flood level _____
2. Move heavy and fragile equipment to low shelves _____
3. Regularly back up electronic files _____
4. Hire a third party to maintain payroll records _____
5. Assign disaster mitigation duties to employees _____
6. Maintain photographic inventories of equipment _____
7. Consider the location of vulnerable equipment _____
8. Periodically evaluate and maintain the building envelope _____

a. so that wind and water don't enter the building.
b. so that your records will be in a secure location.
c. so that they don't fall and break.
d. so that you can file a claim with the insurance company.
e. so that electronic equipment does not suffer water damage.
f. so that you can move it to a safe place in preparation for a natural disaster.
g. so that there's a team ready to take action as soon as disaster strikes.
h. so that your company records are up to date

About you

E React **Answer the questions about the article with your own ideas and opinions.**

1. Which suggestions do you think would be the most useful for businesses in your city or region? Why?

   _____

   _____

2. Which of the suggestions do you think are most difficult for businesses to follow?

   _____

   _____

3. Which suggestions could you use to protect your own personal possessions in the case of a disaster?

   _____

   _____

Writing A report analyzing a problem

A **Complete the report with the expressions in the box. Then circle the correct modal verbs to complete the sentences.**

Another possible reason that	One reason for this
It may also be a result of	This is possibly because

It is now one year since we launched our company website, and the results have not been as good as we had hoped. A lot of potential customers visit the site, but they seem to leave before viewing any of the products that we offer. _____¹ may be the design of the website. The first page that people see is very confusing and **might / would** offer too many choices. As a result, customers **may / could** not take the time to figure out how to navigate to other parts of the site. We could solve this if we had a simpler design. _____² people leave the site so quickly **can / could** be that it isn't updated and refreshed often enough. Nothing puts customers off more than dead links and out-of-date information. We **could / might** plan to update the site on a weekly basis.

Another problem to address is that customers frequently do not complete the ordering process. _____³ it is difficult to find the button you need to click on in order to move to the next page. _____⁴ the complicated "check-out" page, where people have discovered that it **can / could** be difficult to make changes in the order. Customers tell us that problems like these **can / would** be frustrating and deter people from completing their order. This should be fixed as soon as possible, but in the meantime, we **could / may** list our phone number more prominently on the page. It will take some time to fix all of these problems, but it **can / would** be advisable to get started right away. Any changes we make **could / can** have an immediate impact on online sales of our products.

B **Rewrite the second sentences more formally with the expressions given in parentheses. Make any other necessary changes.**

1. Our website often scares people off. Maybe it's the very complicated design. (This may be a result of . . .)

_____

2. Our customers often don't complete their orders. It's very confusing to go through the ordering process. (One reason for this might be . . .)

_____

3. People get very frustrated on our website. Maybe it's because of all the dead links and out-of-date information. (A possible cause could be . . .)

_____

C Editing **Correct the mistakes. One sentence is correct.**

1. If our website had a better design, people can navigate through it more easily.
2. People tell us that they are using our new website and they could find things more easily.
3. I just discovered a great website where you could order foods from all over the world.
4. Some news sites have so many pop-up ads that you could hardly read the articles.
5. One nice thing about the travel site I use is that you can get special discounts on flights.
6. There used to be a site where I can get discounts on designer clothing, but it's gone now.

D **Write a report on a problem that you feel needs attention at your school or place of work. Then check your report for errors.**

Listening extra   Miscommunication in the workplace

A   Which topics do you think would be interesting to learn about? Check (✔) the boxes. Can you think of other topics?

☐ Employee hostility   ☐ Face-to-face communication
☐ Lost productivity   ☐ Email correspondence
☐ Boss–employee relationships   ☐ Problems with the bottom line

B   🔻 Listen to a recording of a training course on workplace miscommunication. Check (✔) the main cause of miscommunication the trainer focuses on.

☐ a. Timing your message badly
☐ b. Using the wrong form of communication
☐ c. Not being a good enough observer
☐ d. Poor listening skills

C   🔻 Listen again. Circle the best options to complete the sentences.

1. According to the speaker, miscommunication is an issue in _____ .
   a. boss–employee relationships   b. knowing people too well   c. staff meetings
2. According to the trainer, the disadvantage of email is that you may not know if employees have _____ your message.
   a. responded to   b. understood   c. read
3. She says that email communication is inefficient because it often requires _____ .
   a. clarification   b. no feedback   c. a fast exchange of messages
4. She says that emails are inefficient because they _____ .
   a. aren't always read   b. take too long to write   c. lead to more emails
5. According to the trainer, bad news is best communicated _____ .
   a. in person   b. electronically   c. in a personal letter
6. Solutions to communication problems are covered in _____ of this program.
   a. the second part   b. every part   c. the last part
7. According to the lecturer, the first step in improving workplace communication is _____ .
   a. taking notes   b. observing behavior   c. doing homework on how to communicate

About you

D   Answer the questions with your own ideas and opinions.

1. Which information in the talk was new or surprising to you? _____
   _____

2. Do you agree with the trainer that face-to-face communication is more effective than email? Why or why not? _____
   _____

3. Have you ever had a problem with miscommunication? What do you think might have caused it? _____
   _____

Relationships

Lesson A **Grammar** Hypothesizing

A **Rewrite the sentences with the underlined *if* clauses. Use the words or structures given.**

STATIONS • ABOUT • SUPPORT • LOG IN • SIGN UP

PODCAST LISTEN LIVE 🎧   👍 | 👎 | 🖨 | ⬚ | SHARE

<u>If you ask any parent about the challenges of a new baby,</u> (imperative) ¹ he or she will have stories to tell. My husband and I are no different. My husband was still in law school when we had our first child. <u>If we had known</u> (Had) ² how difficult it would be to manage a new baby and school, we would have waited. My husband's classes were intense and our daughter was often sick the first few months, so we were both exhausted. <u>If we did it again</u> (Were) ³, we would be better prepared. At that time, I didn't know my new mother-in-law, who lived nearby, very well. <u>If I had been</u> (Had) ⁴ less shy, I might have asked her for help. One day, she happened to call when both the baby and I were sick. She came over in 10 minutes, told me to go to bed, and took care of the baby until I felt better. I was so grateful. After that, I asked her for help a lot. The lesson for new parents is this: Ask for help if you need it. <u>If you don't</u> (Otherwise) ⁵, those first months may be more difficult than necessary.

1. Ask any parent about the challenges of a new baby, and he or she will have stories to tell.
2. _____
3. _____
4. _____
5. _____

B **Complete the sentences with the words in the box. One word is used twice.**

Had	Otherwise	Should	Talk	Were

1. _____ I to start over as a parent, I would learn more about raising a child.
2. _____ I studied child development, I would have understood the different stages that children go through as they grow up.
3. My grandmother once told me, "_____ you think raising children is easy, think again."
4. _____ to any parent and he or she will say that setting boundaries can be difficult.
5. _____ you decide to have a child, it is a good idea to read a book about parenting.
6. Take a class on what to do in a medical emergency. _____ , you might not know how to react if something goes wrong.

About you

C **Think about your experience learning English. Complete the statements with information that is true for you.**

1. Had I known _____ .
2. Were I _____ .
3. Should you _____ .
4. _____ . Otherwise, _____ .

Lesson B Vocabulary Expressions

A Complete the article with the expressions in the box.

above and beyond	sick and tired	stop and think	time and energy	wait and see
give-and-take	sooner or later	success or failure	ups and downs	

Living with roommates

Our college counselor describes some of the problems of living with roommates. She then offers solutions and advice for getting along.

If you _____¹ about it, living with roommates can be a big adjustment. In many cases, you will be living with people that you haven't met before. As a result, in the first few months you have to _____² how well you will get along. Even if you get along pretty well, _____³ you are likely to have a few disagreements.

There will always be _____⁴ when living with different people. Should problems come up between roommates, they can cause a strain on the relationship. For example, one roommate may complain that he or she is _____⁵ of doing more of the chores. If one roommate believes he or she is going _____⁶ what is expected, then there is likely to be resentment.

In order to have a harmonious relationship, there has to be _____⁷. You have to learn to compromise. Building a solid relationship requires work; you have to put in the _____⁸. Overall, the _____⁹ of your relationship depends on each of you adapting to the other.

B Complete the sentences with a word from each box.

and	but	or	age	forth	suffering	think
			energy	later	surely	work

1. In this day _____ , many people don't think they need more relationship advice.
2. If a couple has children, divorce can cause a lot of pain _____ for them.
3. My brother doesn't live _____ in the same city, so he has a long commute.
4. Sooner _____ , most friendships change a little.
5. My grandmother was ill last year. Slowly _____ , she is getting better.
6. If you are not sure what to do, it's a good idea to stop _____ .
7. It takes a lot of time _____ to have a good relationship, but it's worth the effort.
8. It's hard having a long-distance relationship, traveling back _____ to see your partner.

About you

C Answer the questions with your own ideas and opinions.

1. Do you live with roommates or with your family? What issues do you face?

   _____

2. How are relationships different when you live with roommates instead of family?

   _____

3. What advice would you give someone who is having a problem living with a roommate?

   _____

Lesson B Grammar Information focus

A Rewrite the two sentences as one sentence. Keep the clauses in the same order.

RELATIONSHIP
ADVICE
from Dr. Louisa

1. Why do some couples have problems? It's usually obvious.
   <u>Why some couples have problems is usually obvious.</u>

2. What don't many couples understand? Daily communication is necessary.

   _____

3. It's important to agree on this. Where and when can you talk every day?

   _____

4. How do you resolve differences? It can be a big problem.

   _____

5. You should discuss this. How do you express your opinions kindly in an argument?

   _____

6. It's a good idea to decide this. How much free time do you want to spend together?

   _____

7. Should you tell your husband or wife this? Which of his or her hobbies don't you enjoy doing?

   _____

8. You should discuss this. How often do you want to go out separately with your own friends?

   _____

9. It's important to consider this. How much can you compromise in order to accommodate your partner's needs?

   _____

B Unscramble the sentences.

1. do / successful couples / is / What / talk about their problems

   _____ .

2. the success or failure of your relationship / How / helps determine / you communicate

   _____ .

3. can easily become / How many hours / a problem / you work in a week

   _____ .

4. before you get married / whether or not / Discuss / you want to have children

   _____ .

5. where / to live and work / Agree now on / you want

   _____ .

6. is / their child might need independence / What / fail to understand / that / many parents

   _____ .

7. approach problems in / children and parents / their relationship / How / makes a difference

   _____ .

Lesson C Conversation strategies

A Complete the conversations. Write the letters a–e. There is one extra expression.

1. *A* My roommate is driving me crazy.
   B Oh no! What's he doing?
   A Well, _____

2. *A* I'm thinking about joining an online dating site, but I'm nervous about it.
   B Of course you are. It's only natural. I mean, _____

3. *A* Your family is so great. I just can't believe how well you all get along.
   B Well, we do argue, but we never stop speaking or anything, _____

4. *A* Do you think I should take a parenting class?
   B Yeah. Why not? I learned a lot from the one I took.
   A I'm just worried it'll take a lot of time. I don't have much free time.
   B Well, maybe you don't need to take a class. _____

a. in the end, you have to work things out.
b. In a word, she's great.
c. at the end of the day, most people are probably a little anxious at first.
d. When all's said and done, you can probably learn just as much from a book.
e. in a nutshell, he never cleans up.

B Choose the correct options to complete the conversations.

1. *A* My roommate and I really don't get along, so she's moved out.
   B Well, in that case, you'd better work it out. / You don't have to try to work it out, then, do you?

2. *A* My uncle is trying online dating. He's meeting a lot of interesting people.
   B So, in that case, it must be a good way to meet people. / So, he's not likely to meet anyone, then?

3. *A* Not a lot of online dates actually lead to lasting relationships.
   B Really? In that case, it's not ideal if you want to settle down. / It seems like people using online dating sites want long-term relationships, then.

4. *A* It's really hard to meet people. I never meet anyone new.
   B You shouldn't try online dating, then. / In that case, maybe you should try online dating.

5. *A* My best friend is really mad at me for some reason, but I don't know why.
   B You should talk to him, then. / In that case, he'll be really nice to you.

C Complete the conversation with the expressions in the box. Sometimes there is more than one answer.

at the end of the day	✓ in a word	in that case	then

Justina   Guess what? I tried speed dating last weekend.

Samantha   Really? How was it?

Justina   Well, at first I felt really awkward. I mean, I'm pretty shy around new people. ___In a word___,[1] it was hard.

Samantha   So, did you meet anyone, _____[2]?

Justina   Yeah. I met a really nice guy. We're meeting for coffee Friday.

Samantha   Well, _____,[3] maybe I should try it.

Justina   You should! _____,[4] even though it was hard for me, it was worth it.

Samantha   I think I'll try it, _____.[5]

Lesson D Reading Family dinners

A Prepare **Check (✔) the statements that you think are true about family dinners. Then read the article and check your answers.**

1. They can increase children's language skills. _____
2. They do not affect the type of food people eat. _____
3. They may have a positive effect on behavior. _____

THE IMPORTANCE OF FAMILY DINNERS

1 In many of today's households, family dinners have become a thing of the past. With busy schedules held by both parents and children, many families rarely have time to eat dinner together. In recent years, nutrition professionals have been promoting family dinners as research demonstrates the benefits that eating together can provide to family members.

2 You may be wondering, "Why are family dinners so important?" Research has suggested that having dinner as a family on a regular basis has positive effects on the development of adolescents. Family dinners have been linked to a lower risk of obesity, substance abuse, eating disorders, and increased chance of graduating from high school. This document takes a closer look at some of these "dinner dynamics."

CONVERSATION

3 Conversations at the dinner table expand the vocabulary and reading ability of children. This benefit is not dependent on the socioeconomic status of a family; children in all families do better when they engage in dinner conversations. Dinner conversations allow children the opportunity to talk to their parents and siblings and to have an active voice within the family. They also provide opportunities for children to listen to others as well as express their own opinions. Family dinners allow every member of the family a chance to discuss his or her day and share any exciting news.

4 **Suggestions for conversation**
- Discuss the child's day. Ask questions that express your interest in your child's daily life.
- Discuss current events. Bring up news appropriate to the age of your child.
- Pick and choose. Create topics together; write them on a piece of paper and randomly choose one to discuss each night.
- Let all family members talk. Be an active listener and be sure your child learns to listen as well.
- Encourage your child to participate. Do not underestimate your child's ability to hold a conversation.

NUTRITIONAL QUALITY OF THE DIET

5 Eating dinner as a family has been shown to increase the intake of fruits and vegetables, which provide a variety of nutrients and dietary fiber. (For specific food group recommendations at various calorie intakes, visit the website www.mypyramid.gov.) Some studies also have shown that families who eat dinner together tend to eat fewer fried foods and drink less soda. Family meal frequency also is positively linked to the intake of protein, calcium, and some vitamins.

6 **Suggestions for mealtime**
- Make cooking a family activity and include everyone in the preparation process.
- Try fun recipes or old recipes with healthier alternatives.
- Have theme nights such as Italian night, Mexican night, or Caribbean night.
- Create your own original recipes using low-fat ingredients.
- Have family cook-offs.

DEVELOPMENT OF ASSETS

7 Internal assets such as having a positive outlook on personal future and a positive identity are linked to the frequency of family dinners. High-risk behaviors, such as smoking, are less frequent among families who eat meals together more frequently. Concerning boundaries and parental expectations, families who have regular family dinners are more likely to understand, acknowledge, and follow boundaries than those who do not eat dinner together. Self-esteem, motivation, and a decrease in high-risk behaviors are all related to the amount of time spent with family, especially during family dinners.

8 **Final family dinner suggestions**
- Have family dinners at least four to five times a week.
- Turn off TV, radio, MP3 players, and the like during dinner.
- Enjoy positive conversation during the meal.
- Spend at least an hour eating dinner, conversing, and cleaning up together.

SOURCE: University of Florida – Family, Youth, and Community Services

B Read for main ideas **Are the sentences true or false? Write T or F. Correct the false sentences.**

1. Despite people's busy schedules, families frequently eat together. _____
2. Nutrition professionals are encouraging more family dinners nowadays. _____
3. Research links family dinners to healthier weight. _____
4. According to the article, family dinners help children in math. _____
5. The benefits of family dinners depend on one's socioeconomic status. _____
6. Family dinners have been shown to affect the quantities of fruits and vegetables people eat. _____
7. Family dinners do not affect the amount of soda people drink. _____
8. Spending time at dinner with family improves a child's motivation and self-esteem. _____

C Check your understanding **Choose the correct options to complete the sentences. Write a, b, or c.**

1. Suggestions for conversation at family dinners include _____ .
   a. discussing the child's day
   b. discussing current events
   c. both a and b
2. A good way to promote productive conversations at the dinner table is to _____ .
   a. let one person run the conversation
   b. discuss the TV show that is playing while you eat
   c. think of topics ahead of time and then choose one
3. The author suggests that in terms of meal preparation, _____ .
   a. the whole family should prepare a meal together
   b. family members should take take turns preparing meals
   c. the children should prepare a meal for the adults
4. The author emphasizes that the food at family meals should be _____ .
   a. fun
   b. from different parts of the world
   c. healthy
5. Suggestions for successful family dinners include _____ .
   a. spending less than an hour on the meal
   b. turning off all electronics
   c. having family dinners at least twice a week

D Read for details **Complete the sentences with the correct word or phrase from the article.**

1. In modern times, families _____ eat together. (para. 1)
2. Nutrition professionals have been _____ family dinners. (para. 1)
3. Family dinners increase the chance that children will graduate from _____ . (para. 2)
4. Conversations during dinner give children an _____ voice in the family. (para. 3)
5. Family meal frequency is linked to an increase in the _____ of some vitamins. (para. 5)
6. _____ behaviors are less frequent among families who eat meals together. (para. 7)

About you

E React **Answer the questions with your opinions.**

1. Are family dinners important in your culture? Why or why not?

   _____

   _____

2. How has modern life affected family dinners in your culture?

   _____

   _____

Writing Writing a magazine article

A Circle the best options to complete the sentences.

In the last two decades, technology has advanced in **a number of / a great deal of** ways we couldn't have imagined. We can now keep in touch with friends and relatives all around the globe with ease and often at **few / little** cost. By simply posting status updates and new photos online, **a few / a wide variety of** people – from our acquaintances to our closest friends – can receive immediate updates on our lives. One would think that such instantaneous communication would **lead to / effect** closer, stronger relationships. However, researchers have discovered that the growth in social media has resulted **in / to** greater isolation and loneliness for **a great deal of / many** people. For some people, simply having a lot of online friends has **little / few** effect on their sense of feeling connected to the people in their lives. As **a large amount of / several** researchers have noted, nothing can replace the power of face-to-face communication, which has **a range of / a large amount of** positive effects on our well-being.

B Complete the advice column with the expressions in the box.

creates	few	leads	number	result in	several

There are _____¹ strategies that can help people maintain a stable and lasting relationship. Simply following a _____² basic rules can allow your relationship to prosper. First, you should always be honest, as this _____³ to a sense of trust, which is essential for all relationships. Next, it is necessary to be loyal. A _____⁴ of people don't realize that sharing your friends' secrets or talking about them behind their backs can _____⁵ serious problems. Finally, be sure to be generous in your friendship. Avoid selfishness, which _____⁶ the impression that you only care about yourself.

C Editing Correct the error in each sentence.

1. There is a number of situations that can lead to tension in relationships.
2. It takes a great deal time to fully trust someone.
3. A wide range of factors effect how well roommates get along.
4. Most people agree that face-to-face communication leads greater satisfaction.
5. A large number of people is trying online dating these days.
6. It only takes a few effort to be a respectful roommate.
7. There is various ways that you can improve any relationship.
8. There are a number of factors that makes family dinners more enjoyable for everyone.

D Write a short magazine article in which you offer advice for the following situation. Check your work for errors.

My roommate is so noisy. She's constantly talking loudly on the phone, even when I'm trying to study. Then, when I'm just about to go to sleep, she turns on the TV. Sometimes she invites friends over late at night. I'm really frustrated. What should I do?

Listening extra Relationship troubles

A Read the relationship problems that people might talk about on an advice radio show. Write two more possible problems.

The caller . . .

☐ 1. has a difficult assistant.
☐ 2. has a boss who's unpredictable.
☐ 3. can't understand a professor.
☐ 4. wants to help a roommate.
☐ 5. has an annoying roommate.
☐ 6. has problems with a family member.
☐ 7. _____
☐ 8. _____

B 🔽 Listen to the radio show. Check (✔) the problems from Exercise A that are discussed.

C 🔽 Listen again. Are the sentences true or false? Write T or F.

1. Dr. Borgo has been practicing psychology for more than 25 years. _____
2. Sally's boss's mood is unpredictable. _____
3. Dr. Borgo advises Sally not to take her boss's criticism personally. _____
4. Dr. Borgo suggests that Sally get clear instructions from her boss about her work. _____
5. Dr. Borgo believes Sally's problem can be easily resolved. _____
6. Tarek's roommate has a habit of leaving his stuff around. _____
7. Tarek gives examples about his roommate with food, headphones, and a laptop. _____
8. Dr. Borgo advises Tarek to find another roommate. _____
9. Camilla wants more freedom and independence. _____
10. Dr. Borgo advises Camilla to call her mother a lot to resolve the issue. _____

D 🔽 Listen again. Complete the sentences with two words.

1. Dr. Borgo says Sally should approach her situation _____ _____ .
2. He advises Sally to remain professional and positive regardless of her boss's _____ _____ .
3. When Tarek couldn't find his laptop he _____ _____ and called campus security.
4. Dr. Borgo advises that in his conversation with his roommate, Tarek shouldn't bring up _____ _____ .
5. Camilla's mother calls her about _____ _____ a day.
6. Camilla should tell her mother that she wants her in her life, but she needs _____ _____ .

About you **E** Give your opinion. Do you agree with the advice for each person? Do you think it will solve the problems? Why or why not?

1. Sally: _____

_____

2. Tarek: _____

_____

3. Camilla: _____

_____

Now complete the *Unit 7 Progress chart* on page 100.

History

Lesson A Grammar Referring to past time

A Complete the article. Use the verbs given and perfect infinitives. Some verbs are passive.

I _____¹ (would like / meet) Martin Luther King, Jr., the American
clergyman and social activist. He _____² (widely acknowledge / advance)
civil rights in American society through his program of nonviolent civil
disobedience. A brilliant communicator, his famous anti-racism speech,
"I have a dream," delivered on August 28, 1963, _____³ (said / establish)
him as one of the greatest orators in American history. In terms of concrete
change, his main legacy _____⁴ (consider / be) the passing of the Civil
Rights Act of 1968, which prohibited racial discrimination in the U.S. His work
_____⁵ (also know / influence) the Black Consciousness Movement, which
fought for civil rights in South Africa. His life certainly _____⁶ (seem / have)
an impact on the American people. Hundreds of streets have been named in
his honor, and he will always be celebrated on the third Monday of January –
Martin Luther King, Jr. Day.

B Rewrite the sentences so they make sense by adding a perfect infinitive.

1. Many human rights activists would like to discuss passive resistance with Mahatma Gandhi.
   _____

2. According to Nostradamus, the sixteenth century prophet, the world is supposed to come
   to an end on December 21st, 2012.
   _____

3. Sir Isaac Newton's 1687 work, "Mathematical Principles of Natural Philosophy" is said to
   lay the foundations for most of classical mechanics.
   _____

4. Jack Nicklaus is more than a great golfer – he happens to win 18 major championships.
   _____

5. As an art student, I would love to watch Leonardo da Vinci create one of his masterpieces.
   _____

6. Singapore statesman Lee Kuan Yew is acknowledged to help trigger the Asian economic miracle.
   _____

About you

C Answer the questions with your own opinions.

1. Imagine you were alive 200 years ago. Which famous figure would you like to have met? Why?
   _____

2. Who is acknowledged to have been an influential leader in your country? Why?
   _____

Lesson B Vocabulary Inventions that changed the world

A **Replace the words in bold with words from the box with similar meanings.**

| apparent | gradual | lasting | profound | ✓significant | universal | visible |

THE HISTORY BUFF

Vaccinations to stop the spread of disease have resulted in **important** significant[1] changes to our quality of life. Although the benefits are **slow to observe** _____[2] and not immediately **obvious** _____[3], vaccination campaigns have had a **deep** _____[4] and **ongoing** _____[5] impact on public health. Polio has become much less **conspicuous** _____[6], for example, and enhanced vaccination efforts could result in the **global** _____[7] eradication of many diseases.

B **Circle the correct words to complete the article.**

It used to be only the elite who could read, but the invention of the printing press in 1450 marked the beginning of mass communication and a **rapid / minor** increase in literacy rates. **Universal / Minute** access to new ideas undermined the entrenched authority of the church and caused **a major / an imperceptible** shift from religious to political power in Western Europe. The printing press also facilitated the **slight / massive** benefits of the scientific revolution, made possible by the sharing of information in scientific publishing.

C **Complete the article with the words in the box that have similar meanings to the words given in parentheses.**

| immediate | insignificant | local | long-term | sudden | superficial | temporary |

Compared to the sophisticated electronics in our homes, the humble plow may seem like an _____[1] (not important) invention. Yet the invention of the plow had a profound effect on humanity, and its impact was far from _____[2] (on the surface). An _____[3] (instant) benefit was that the process of growing food became easier and faster, and people could harvest more food than they needed. This led to a _____[4] (fast) change in human lifestyle. It freed up time for other activities, like trading _____[5] (from the area) products for other goods and services. These activities of storing and trading materials had profound, _____[6] (for a long time) benefits for civilization, driving – amongst other things – the invention of writing and number systems. While the plow was a _____[7] (not permanent) feature of history, its effects spread beyond agriculture.

About you

D **Write about an invention that you think has had the greatest universal impact and why.**

_____

_____

Lesson B Grammar Giving ideas extra focus

A Complete the cleft sentences using *it*, a correct form of *be*, and *who* or *that*. Some sentences are negative. Sometimes there is more than one possible answer.

This winter we will celebrate "On this day in history" by commemorating scientists who made significant discoveries.

FEBRUARY 19, 1473 On this day in history, Nicolas Copernicus was born.

_____[1] Copernicus _____[2] educated the world about astronomy. _____[3] until his studies were published in 1543 _____[4] a centuries-old belief was dispelled. Copernicus demonstrated in mathematical terms why _____[5] the sun, and not Earth, _____[6] sits at the center of our solar system. This was a major discovery, and _____[7] his work in astronomy _____[8] is often cited as the beginning of modern science.

DECEMBER 25, 1642 On this day in history, Sir Isaac Newton was born.

_____[1] thanks to Sir Isaac Newton _____[2] we understand the concept of gravity. _____[3] only when he explained its laws _____[4] we understood why objects fall down, and what draws them toward each other. While _____[5] gravity and the laws of motion _____[6] he is most famous for, his other discoveries are also significant. For example, _____[7] Newton _____[8] constructed the first reflecting telescope.

B Rewrite the sentences as cleft sentences with *it + be*. Add emphasis to the words or phrases that are underlined.

SEPTEMBER 22, 1791 On this day in history, Michael Faraday was born.

1. Electricity makes our lives easier <u>thanks to Michael Faraday</u>.

   _____

2. <u>His discovery</u> of using electricity and a magnet to rotate a wire led to the development of the electric motor.

   _____

3. <u>Faraday</u> became the first person to produce an electric current by moving a wire through a magnetic field.

   _____

4. Electricity became practical for use in technology <u>largely due to his efforts</u>.

   _____

About you

C Answer the questions about the three scientists and their discoveries with your own opinions.

1. Which of these scientists do you think is most notable? Why?

   _____

   _____

2. Which of these discoveries do you think had the greatest impact on our lives? Why?

   _____

   _____

Lesson C Conversation strategies

A Add the sentences in the box to the conversation. Then complete the expressions in bold to avoid talking about certain topics. Sometimes there is more than one possible answer.

> That's always a big debate in our class.
> I can't believe how they just accept one view.
>
> I'm dreading my history class.
> I feel like that, too.

Mike _____¹ I know I'm going to argue about today's reading with this one guy in the class.

Kate Why's that? Do you have very different opinions?

Mike **Don't** _____²! Let's just say that he has a really narrow outlook on life.

Kate I have people like that in my history class, too. _____³. It's like they're afraid to consider other points of view.

Mike Yes, especially on things like foreign policy. _____⁴. But anyway, **let's not** _____⁵. It just frustrates me.

Kate Yeah, I know how you feel. _____⁶. It's like people can't accept that sometimes our leaders got things wrong! But as you say, **that's a** _____⁷.

Mike Yeah, **I'd rather** _____⁸. I have enough of that in my history class!

B Choose the most appropriate response to end each conversation. Write the letters a–d. There are two extra responses.

1. *A* I can't understand why so few students choose history as a subject. It's so important to our understanding of the world.
   B A lot of students think it's just about learning facts. But it's about much more than that.
   A _____

2. *A* Have you noticed how place names on a map often reflect a country's history?
   B Well, most places in my country have Anglo-Saxon or Celtic names.
   A _____

> a. Exactly. That's what I'm saying. It shows that different cultures dominated at different times.
> b. Right. That's what I'm saying. I don't accept that this is the most peaceful period in human history.
> c. That's what I'm saying. It gives you a real insight into who we are and why we behave the way we do.
> d. Yes, that's what I mean. I'm always wary of history that gives just one side of the story.

C Circle the best option to complete the conversation. Sometimes both are correct.

A If you look at history, wars often start because countries want what other countries have. You know, maybe a world government would solve that problem.

B <u>Don't get me started</u> / <u>That's what I'm saying</u>. There's no way it would work. Different cultures will always protect their interests.

A <u>That's what I'm saying.</u> / <u>Let's not go there</u>. Having no borders means there's no need to protect resources. They would belong to everyone.

B I just don't think it would work. I mean, imagine trying to elect just one world leader! Impossible. <u>But that's another story.</u> / <u>That's what I mean</u>.

A Well, <u>I'd rather not talk about it.</u> / <u>That's what I'm saying</u>. Let's talk about something else.

Lesson D Reading California Gold Rush

A **Prepare** **Which of these statements about the California Gold Rush do you think are true? Check (✔) the statements.**

1. ☐ The Gold Rush began in 1949.
2. ☐ Anybody who found gold during the Gold Rush period could keep it.
3. ☐ The Levi Strauss company began during the Gold Rush.
4. ☐ A third of all Gold Rush prospectors were dead within six months of arriving in California.

B **Read for main ideas** **Read the article. Which of the statements in Exercise A are true?**

GOING TO CALIFORNIA: 49ers and the Gold Rush

1 James Marshall found gold while working for John Sutter at his ranch in Northern California on January 24, 1848. He had been hired to build a mill for Sutter. This place would enter American lore as "Sutter's Mill." Word quickly spread through California, the rest of America, and eventually the world, and people flocked to California to make their fortune. Many of the gold seekers came from as far away as Latin America and China. In fact, according to some estimates, the population increased by 86,000 people in two years. Most of these treasure seekers left for California in 1849, hence our name for them: 49ers. Many of the 49ers themselves picked an appropriate name from Greek mythology: Argonauts. These Argonauts were in search of their own form of a golden fleece – wealth free for the taking. The trek was arduous for those who came over land. ¹☐ It could sometimes take up to nine months to get to California. For the immigrants who came from across the ocean, San Francisco became the most popular port of call. In fact, San Francisco's population grew from about 800 in 1848 to over 50,000 in 1849. As a result of this growth, new towns, roads, schools, and churches were built.

2 The first lucky arrivals were able to find nuggets of gold in the streambeds. These people made quick fortunes. ²☐ It was a unique time in history where individuals with literally nothing to their name could become extremely wealthy. The gold was free for whoever was lucky enough to find it. It is no surprise that gold fever hit so heavily. Yet the majority of those who made the trek out West were not so lucky. The individuals who became the richest were in fact not these early miners, but were instead entrepreneurs who created businesses to support all of the prospectors. ³☐ It is easy to think of all the essentials this mass of humanity would need in order to live. Businesses sprang up to meet their needs. Some of these businesses are still around today, including Levi Strauss and Wells Fargo.

3 The individuals who made their way out West during the Gold Rush met with numerous hardships. After making the journey, they often found the work to be extremely hard with no guarantee of success. Further, the death rate was very high. ⁴☐ According to Steve Wiegard, staff writer for the *Sacramento Bee*, "one in every five miners who came to California in 1849 was dead within six months." Lawlessness and racism were rampant. However, the impact of the Gold Rush on American history cannot be overestimated.

4 The Gold Rush reinforced the idea of Manifest Destiny. America was destined to span from Atlantic to Pacific, and the accidental discovery of gold made California an even more essential part of the picture. ⁵☐ California was admitted as the 31st state in the union in 1850.

SOURCE: www.americanhistory.com

C Information flow **Find the correct places in the article for these sentences. Write the letters a–e in the boxes.**

a. Miners faced possible starvation or the contraction of a disease.

b. Known as the "Golden State," California represented a place where someone could start a new life and become rich.

c. Many made their journey on foot or by wagon.

d. Gold worth millions of dollars was found by a few miners.

e. For example, Samuel Brannan became one of the richest men by opening shops and selling newspapers.

D Read for main ideas **Are the sentences true or false, or is the information not given in the article? Write, T, F, or NG. Correct the false sentences.**

1. John Sutter found gold while working on James Marshall's ranch in Northern California. _____
2. James Marshall was obligated to share his gold with John Sutter. _____
3. The miners called themselves Argonauts after a group of adventurers from Greek mythology. _____
4. San Francisco's population grew rapidly during the Gold Rush because of all the new building there. _____
5. Early gold miners needed to acquire a license to dig for gold. _____
6. Most of the 49ers had no knowledge or experience of mining gold. _____
7. Only the lucky few who found big gold deposits became rich during the Gold Rush. _____
8. There was very little crime in the mines. _____
9. The miners generally worked 12 hours per day, 7 days a week. _____
10. The term Manifest Destiny refers to a belief that America would inevitably spread from the east side of the continent to the west. _____

E **Circle the correct options to complete the sentences.**

1. The gold miners were called 49ers because they _____ in 1949.
   a. set out for California   b. first found gold   c. arrived in California
2. The population in San Francisco grew to _____ in 1949.
   a. over 86,000   b. more than 50,000   c. around 800
3. The article describes this time as unique because it was the first time people _____ .
   a. became rich quickly   b. emigrated   c. found gold
4. The miners who went to the West all found _____ .
   a. gold   b. difficulties   c. jobs
5. The impact that the Gold Rush had on American history _____ .
   a. is often overestimated   b. was not significant c. was enormous

About you **F** React **Answer the questions with your own views.**

1. What did you find most interesting about the article?

   _____

   _____

2. What did you find surprising about the article?

   _____

   _____

3. Describe a major event in your country's history.

   _____

   _____

Writing Writing a narrative

A Circle the correct expressions to complete the narrative.

ABOUT US

INTERVIEWS

NARRATIVES

TIMELINES

CONTACT ME

Prior to World War II, my great-grandparents, Frank and Louise, married and were living in London. **As soon as / On** the war started, my great-grandmother discovered that she was pregnant, but, unfortunately, my great-grandfather was called to the war front six months later. My great-grandmother was **subsequent / subsequently** forced to evacuate London. Soon after **arrived / arriving** at her new residence, she had a baby girl. Sadly, three weeks later, she had news that my great-grandfather had been killed in the war. Deeply **saddened / sad** by this, she decided to give up the baby for adoption. **Once / On** the war ended, she returned to London where she had **previously / previous** lived with Frank and tried to find her daughter. However, in those days, it just wasn't possible. **Resigned / Resigning** to this, she married again and eventually had four more children – a girl and three boys. She died in 1992.

In the late 1990s, my grandmother was invited to be an audience member in a TV show. **Excited / Exciting** by the opportunity, she went along with her three brothers. They were amazed to discover that their half sister had contacted the show, **hoping / hoped** to find any siblings. **In the end / At the end**, all of my great-grandmother's children were reunited and the sisters became great friends.

B Rewrite the sentences with the words given and make any other necessary changes.

My great-grandfather left Italy for the United States in 1887.
1. He arrived at Ellis Island and then he was given a new last name. (on)
2. He settled in, then looked for a job and found one washing dishes in a restaurant. (once / eventually)
3. He bought a book to teach himself English when he had saved enough money. (as soon as)
4. He became the restaurant manager and that marked the beginning of a successful era for the restaurant. (after a while / participle clause)
5. He started his own restaurant, which my family still owns today. (in the end)

C Editing **Correct the errors with *finally, at the end,* or *in the end*.**

1. In the end of the war, my great-grandmother tried to find her daughter.
2. My great-aunt wanted to find her birth family, and thanks to the TV show, she at the end found her siblings.
3. At the end, the family members were reunited.
4. In the end of the TV show, the brothers and sisters exchanged contact details and promised never to lose touch.

D Interview a family member or friend. Write a narrative account of an interesting event in his or her life. Check your work for errors.

Listening extra The history of English

A **How much do you know about the history of English? Check (✔) the statements that you think are true.**

- ☐ 1. English has been developing for thousands of years.
- ☐ 2. French has been a major influence on English.
- ☐ 3. The Modern English era began in the nineteenth century.
- ☐ 4. There are three recognized varieties of English.
- ☐ 5. English has recently become resistant to change.

The gray countries show where English is spoken as the primary language.

B 📥 **Listen to the podcast about the history of English. Which of the statements in Exercise A are correct?**

C 📥 **Listen again. Are the sentences true or false? Write T or F.**

1. The early origins of English can be traced to Denmark and northern Germany. _____
2. About 20 percent of modern English words originate from Old English. _____
3. At one point, English was the language of the lower class in England. _____
4. The word *décor* was absorbed into English during the Modern English period. _____
5. We owe the standardization of English grammar and spelling to the Industrial Revolution. _____
6. The different varieties of English owe their existence to the British Empire. _____
7. Movies are one reason why American English is influential today. _____
8. These days, it's only technology that adds new words to English. _____
9. It's a fact that all languages are constantly evolving. _____
10. In the future, people might not understand the English we speak today. _____

D 📥 **Listen again and complete the sentences with the missing words.**

1. People from Denmark and northern Germany went to England _____ thousand years ago.
2. _____ years ago the French invaded England.
3. English became dominant again by the _____ century.
4. Modern English is divided into _____ time periods.
5. The Late Modern English period can be traced back to about the year _____ .

About you

E **Answer the questions with your own ideas and opinions.**

1. Have any of the words from your native language become commonly used in English?

_____

_____

2. How has your first language been affected by outside influences?

_____

_____

3. Are there different varieties of your first language, as there are with English? What are some differences between them?

_____

_____

Now complete the Unit 8 Progress chart on page 100.   Unit 8: History   **65**

9

Engineering wonders

Lesson A Grammar Unknown people and things

A **Circle the correct words to complete the posting on a career advice website.**

Job Profiles
Education Guide
  search by state
  search by field
Career Resources
  Career planning
  Relocating
  Interviewing
  Salary negotiating
  Work at home
  Retirement
Contact Us

CAREERS IN ENGINEERING

software_gal:

When I was a teenager, **whenever / however** I spent long hours at my computer, my friends would call me a "computer geek." I loved computers, so it was natural for me to major in software engineering in college. After graduating, I realized that there were jobs for software engineers everywhere, and I could move **whatever / wherever** I wanted to. I chose a company in Northern California because it gave me the freedom to work **wherever / whatever** I chose – from home, in the office, or even outdoors in the company garden! Furthermore, if no meetings are scheduled, I can begin work **whenever / whoever** I want and finish **however / whenever** late I want. As long as I put in 35 hours a week, I can follow **whatever / whenever** schedule suits me. I love my work and **whatever / whenever** a teenager with an interest in math and science asks me for career advice, I always mention computer science and software engineering. **Whoever / Whichever** said that it was boring to be a computer geek was wrong. Software engineering has turned out to be an exciting career for me.

B **Complete the conversation with -*ever* words. Sometimes there is more than one answer.**

A When I graduate, I'm going to study to be either a civil or an architectural engineer.

B Well, _____¹ field you choose, there'll be a lot of job opportunities. I mean, _____² you look these days – on the Internet, or company websites – you see ads for engineers. But engineering is kind of a difficult course of study.

A I know. But I'll do _____³ it takes to get into a good engineering program.

B Do you have a program in mind? Your grades are good, so I'm sure _____⁴ you decide to go for your degree, you'll get a good scholarship.

A Really? _____⁵ I ask about scholarships at school, they say they're hard to get.

B Well, _____⁶ told you that is wrong, especially in the field of engineering.

A That's good to know. Maybe with a scholarship I could afford to go to a really good school, and if I still need more money, I suppose I could work part-time.

B Well, _____⁷ you decide to pay for it all, I'm sure things will work out for you.

About you

C **Answer the questions with your own opinions.**

1. What field of engineering do you find the most interesting? Why?

_____

_____

2. Do you think it is worthwhile to pursue a career in engineering? Why or why not?

_____

_____

Lesson B Vocabulary Incredible feats

A **Replace the words in bold with expressions from the box that have similar meanings.**

ahead of schedule	constructed	erected	installed	positioned
assembled	delayed	✓ in a short time frame	maneuvered	

Incredible engineering projects

1. The Egyptian Pyramids of Giza, which are over 4,000 years old, were built **extremely quickly** ___in a short time frame___ , taking as few as 23 years from start to finish, according to some scholars. A big mystery is how the heavy stones were **skillfully moved** _____ into position by manual laborers, which was an incredible engineering feat.

2. The longest engineering project in history is the Great Wall of China, which was **built** _____ over a period of 2,000 years.

3. To avoid building directly on unstable permafrost, Chinese engineers raised the tracks of the Qinzang railway far above ground and sank the foundations deep into the mountain. Incredibly, this challenging project was never **stopped or slowed down** _____ . In fact, it was finished in 2006, three years **earlier than planned** _____ .

4. In 1885, the Statue of Liberty was transported from France as 300 copper sheets, which were then **put together** _____ in New York City. The sheets were hung on a metal frame that had been **raised** _____ on a large stone pedestal. The sculptor, Auguste Bartholdi, **carefully placed** _____ the torch in the statue's right hand. In 1909, an elevator was **put in place** _____ for tourists.

B **Complete the paragraph with the words in the box. Sometimes more than one fits.**

ahead of schedule	concrete	erected	in a short time frame	steel
completed on time	constructed	fell behind schedule	installed	

The world's tallest structures, 1889–1972

The Eiffel Tower was _____[1] between 1887 and 1889 to serve as an entrance to the 1889 World's Fair in Paris. At 300 meters (986 feet), it was the tallest structure in the world for 41 years, until the Chrysler Building was _____[2] in New York City in 1930. Towards the end of construction, the project _____[3]. Thus the tower was not open to the public until nine days after the start of the fair. In addition, although the elevators, had been put in place and _____[4] the work on them was not _____[5], so at first visitors had to ascend the tower by foot. It nevertheless was an incredible success, attracting almost two million visitors during the fair.

When the Chrysler Building opened, it was 319 meters (1,046 feet) high, but it held the record for height for only one year. In 1931, the Empire State Building was finished, and at 381 meters (1,250 feet) it remained the world's tallest structure for 41 years, until 1972. The innovative construction process included erecting a _____[6] frame that was then covered with _____[7] to make it stronger and to protect against fire. It was built _____[8] taking only 1 year and 45 days. The original plan was to construct it in 18 months, so it was actually completed _____[9].

Lesson B Grammar Emphasizing ideas

A Circle the correct options to complete the paragraph.

BUILDING THE

BURJ KHALIFA,

THE TALLEST
BUILDING
IN THE WORLD

In 2004, when engineers began to build Burj Khalifa in Dubai, **they had / did they have** many obstacles to overcome. Never before **they had / had they** attempted to build a structure 829 meters (2,722 feet) high. In the previous 30 years, **engineers had / had engineers** constructed only five skyscrapers over 400 meters high, and the tallest of these, Taipei 101, was only 509 meters. Furthermore, **the site posed / did the site pose** several challenges. Not only **the soil was / was the soil** on the site somewhat unstable, there were also intense winds. For these reasons **the foundation was / was the foundation** carefully designed to distribute the weight of the 163-story building broadly over the site. In addition, **a Y-shaped floor plan was devised / was devised a Y-shaped floor plan** to withstand the extremely high winds. Only after conducting 40 wind tunnel tests **the engineers felt / did the engineers feel** confident that the structure could withstand major weather events. The floor plan had an additional benefit – not only **it solved / did it solve** the wind problem, it also maximized tenants' views of the Persian Gulf. With complete confidence **the team began / did the team begin** construction in 2004, with plans to open the building in 2009. Little **they knew / did they know** that a global economic crisis in 2007 would delay the project. Fortunately, **the financial obstacles were / were the financial obstacles** overcome, and the building was opened to great fanfare in 2010. It now attracts businesses, tenants, and tourists from all over the world.

B Rewrite each sentence starting with the words provided.

Not every engineering project goes smoothly. The Central Artery / Tunnel Project in Boston, also known as the "Big Dig," was truly a feat of engineering, but construction was plagued with problems.

1. Such a large urban highway project had never been undertaken in the United States.
   Never before _____ .
2. When excavation began in 1991, the planners didn't know that the project wouldn't be done until 2007.
   When excavation began in 1991, little _____ .
3. They also didn't imagine that it would cost $18 billion more than projected.
   Nor _____ .
4. The project was over budget, and there were also many construction problems.
   Not only _____ .
5. Highway projects rarely have so many problems with the quality of materials and construction.
   Rarely _____ .
6. Some of the concrete was defective, and the tunnel light fixtures started to fall down.
   Not only _____ .
7. The lighting problem was solved by replacing all 2,500 light fixtures.
   Only by _____ .
8. The project is now complete, and the "Big Dig" is no longer the main topic of conversation in Boston.
   The project is now complete, and no longer _____ .

Lesson C Conversation strategies

A Circle the best options to complete the conversation. Sometimes both are correct.

Professor   Today we're going to talk about engineering priorities for the twenty-first century. And the first thing I'd like to do is to get your opinions on what these priorities should be. . . .

Sun-hee   Well, **given / in light of** our current energy needs, I would say that developing solar power is a major priority.

Pierre   Right. But a bigger priority is to prepare for extreme weather, isn't it, especially **in light of the fact that / considering** what we know about rising sea levels?

Ana   OK, but don't we need a comprehensive plan to address climate change, **in view of the fact that / considering that** we may not be able to keep ahead of the weather problems?

Somsak   I agree. **Given that / In light of** all the predictions about the future, we have to do whatever we can to turn the weather situation around.

Ayshe   You know, whenever the topic of priorities comes up, everyone talks about climate change, but what are we doing about clean water? I mean, **given that / in view of** 800 million people in the world today lack access to clean water, we can't ignore the problem.

Rashid   No, but **in view of / considering the fact that** all the challenges we face, how can we prioritize? Shouldn't we try to address all the problems at the same time?

B Complete these comments with the expressions in the box. Then add *at all* or *whatsoever*.

no doubt	no effect	no interest	no need	no sense	nothing

1. We have _____ for new highway projects. It just means more cars and more pollution.
2. It makes _____ to build on the seacoast given all the flooding we've had.
3. Many companies seem to have _____ in protecting the environment.
4. Some people do _____ to conserve energy. They're just not concerned.
5. There seems to be _____ that the climate is changing. Approximately 97 percent of climate experts agree on that.
6. People protest about pollution and environment problems, but it has _____ .

C Complete the conversations with expressions in the box. More than one answer is possible and some expressions are used more than once.

at all	considering	given that	in light of	in view of the fact that	whatsoever

1. *A* It bothers me that some countries do nothing _____ to address climate change.
   B Actually, I think most countries have taken some action, but _____ the potential dangers, they obviously should do more.

2. *A* I hear that they're proposing to increase the number of nuclear plants, you know, _____ nuclear power is supposedly cleaner than gas or oil.
   B You're kidding! I mean, _____ all the nuclear accidents we've had recently, that doesn't make any sense to me _____ .

3. *A* Sometimes I have my doubts about the safety of these new high-speed trains, _____ there have been so many serious accidents lately.
   B Actually, I have no doubts about them _____ . They're extremely safe compared to cars and buses.

Lesson D Reading Robots

A Prepare **What kinds of jobs do you think computers and robots will take over in the future? Check (✔) the boxes. Then read the article. Does the article present the same ideas?**

☐ barbershop   ☐ call center   ☐ clerical   ☐ healthcare   ☐ managerial

Robots are taking mid-level jobs, changing the economy

1 Computers and robots will replace humans in enough jobs that they will dramatically change the economy, said industry watchers and MIT economists at a robotics symposium Monday. And, they said, the transition has already started.

2 "What we're finally seeing is that our digital helpers aren't just catching up to us, but, in some cases, are passing us," said Andrew McAfee, an MIT economist and co-author of the book *Race Against the Machine*. "In some head-to-head contests, machines have raced past us."

3 Speaking at the symposium at MIT, McAfee noted that IBM's Watson supercomputer recently bested human champions on the *Jeopardy* game show. A Google self-driving car has been coursing around California, and the military is using robots on the ground and in the air in combat zones.

4 "We thought human beings held the high ground in a lot of these areas," McAfee said. "We looked around and suddenly saw computers doing things they weren't supposed to be good at. . . . We're going to see computers, robots doing a lot of jobs that humans are holding today."

5 But humans needn't get nervous.

6 McAfee isn't saying robots are about to become our managers. They're not going to run companies or hold department meetings. However, they will be replacing people in company call centers. They'll also be doing financial and industry analysis and a lot of mid-level kinds of jobs that people are paid to do today.

7 "There's a shift in how work gets done and how wealth is allocated," said Erik Brynjolfsson, director of the MIT Center for Digital Business. "Not so many people will be needed to work at H&R Block now that there's software to do our taxes."

8 Some jobs will be fairly safe at least for the foreseeable future, according to David Autor, an MIT economist. Autor said that low-skilled and low-paying jobs, such as dog groomers, restaurant wait staff, and barbers, should be safe. Those are jobs that would be tough for computers or robots to take on.

9 High-skilled, high-paying jobs, such as high-technology workers and healthcare providers, should also be safe.

10 The shift is going to come in the middle of the workforce, Autor said. Mid-level paying jobs requiring mid-levels of education are in danger of being lost to technology.

11 "Think clerical and administrative support," he added. "Support and file and copy are more and more being done by machinery. . . . This is not unique to the United States, which makes it important as an [economic and global] phenomenon. In every country, middle jobs are contracting."

12 However, Autor said it's a fallacy that there's only a certain amount of work to be done and that machines will eliminate all jobs and leave people with nothing to do.

13 "Technology doesn't eliminate jobs altogether," he said. "And it does raise wealth. But it doesn't always have a positive distribution. . . . We shouldn't be worried that we're going to run out of jobs, but we may not like all the jobs being created. It's something we should be paying attention to."

B Paraphrase **The article presents six major ideas about technological change. Which ideas are presented in the paragraphs? Match the paragraphs and ideas. Write the letters a–e.**

> a. Technology won't replace all jobs, but it may create some undesirable jobs.
> b. Technological change is causing a global decrease in mid-level jobs.
> c. Computers are increasingly doing jobs we thought only humans could do.
> d. Computers and robots aren't replacing high- or low-skilled jobs, only mid-level jobs.

1. Paragraphs 2–4 _____   3. Paragraphs 10–11 _____
2. Paragraphs 5–9 _____   4. Paragraphs 12–13 _____

C Read for detail **Circle the correct options to complete the sentences.**

1. The robotics symposium heard that the use of computers and robots _____
   a. will not significantly influence the economy in the future.
   b. is already impacting the economy.
   c. has radically changed the economy already.

2. Computers are starting to do things that only humans were supposed to be able to do, such as _____
   a. operate vehicles.
   b. initiate military conflict.
   c. host game shows.

3. One thing people predict computers won't be doing is _____
   a. answering customer service calls.
   b. managing companies.
   c. helping people calculate their taxes.

4. The jobs that are most in danger of being eliminated are now those that require _____
   a. advanced education and skills.
   b. a mid-level education.
   c. little schooling or training.

5. Some people who are likely to lose their jobs are _____
   a. software developers.
   b. doctors and nurses.
   c. clerical and administrative staff.

6. According to David Autor, technology affects the job market by _____
   a. getting rid of jobs completely.
   b. generating less wealth.
   c. creating jobs we may not necessarily like.

About you

D React **Answer the questions with your own opinions.**

1. Which of the changes, if any, as described in the article do you see happening around you?

   _____

   _____

   _____

2. What do you see as the potential dangers of the increasing use of robots?

   _____

   _____

   _____

Writing A classification essay

A **Complete the essay with the expressions in the box. Use capital letters if necessary.**

another type	the first type	there are a number of
can be classified by	the second type	yet another type

Thanks to technological advances, _____¹ different types of robots.
Robots _____² the types of jobs they perform. _____³
is the rescue robot, which can save people in danger, such as after an earthquake.
Clearly, they are useful for accessing places that are too dangerous for humans.
_____⁴ is the domestic robot, which carries out tasks around the
house, like vacuuming. _____⁵ is the mobile robot, which has the ability to move
around as it performs tasks. These have started to replace workers in factories and are popular in the
military. _____⁶ of robot is used for medical purposes to assist with surgery and
other medical procedures.

B **Combine the sentences with the expressions given. Make any necessary changes.**

The Palm Islands, in the United Arab Emirates, were artificially created by civil and marine engineers.

1. When creating the islands, the engineers used natural materials like rocks and sand. (as a
    substitute for) They did not use more traditional construction materials like concrete and steel.

    _____

    _____

2. To build the foundation of the islands, the marine engineers decided to use calcified rock
    from under the seabed. (instead of) They were going to use desert sand.

    _____

    _____

3. Engineers created 16 channels to allow water to circulate because they wanted clean,
    flowing water around the islands. (as opposed to) They didn't want stagnant water.

    _____

    _____

4. Because there was so little time in the schedule, the engineers made all their decisions on
    the job. (rather than) They did not research the project ahead of time.

    _____

    _____

C Editing **Correct the error in each sentence. One sentence is correct.**

1. Robots are better at some rescue efforts rather than humans.
2. It makes sense to send robots rather than humans into dangerous situations to save lives.
3. The military would rather prefer to use robots in many types of combat situations.
4. The police and the military use robots, as opposed for humans, to dismantle bombs.
5. "Virtual" robots are used as an alternative of humans to search the Web.
6. For certain tasks, people would rather have a human rather than a robot.
7. Most people would want a human server in a restaurant rather than to have a robot.
8. In many cases, robots simply cannot substitute to humans.

D **Write a classification essay about different fields of engineering. Then check for errors.**

Listening extra A student presentation

A **Match the words and their definitions. Write the letters a–d.**

1. the coast _____
2. a river delta _____
3. storm surge barriers, sea walls, dikes _____
4. an estuary _____

a. land where a river divides before flowing into a sea or ocean
b. where a river joins a sea or ocean
c. the land next to a sea or ocean
d. structures that protect the land from sea or ocean waves

B 🔽 **Listen to a student presentation about the Delta Works in the Netherlands. Then circle the best option to complete the sentences.**

1. Over the past 1,000 years, the Netherlands has developed a vast system of dikes because _____ .
   a. 20 percent of its coast is on the North Sea
   b. the entire country is below sea level
   c. two-thirds of its land is at risk of flooding
2. The Delta Works was initiated as a reaction to _____ .
   a. an unusually devastating flood
   b. predictions of climate change
   c. a global interest in flood control
3. The Delta Works provides _____ protection for the people of the coastal area.
   a. the only
   b. extra
   c. little
4. Two of the sea barriers remain open except when _____ .
   a. the water is three meters above sea level
   b. the tide goes out
   c. the sea water comes in
5. The international reaction to the Delta Works project has been to _____ .
   a. learn from it
   b. ignore it
   c. criticize it

C 🔽 **Listen again and complete the facts and figures.**

1. In the Netherlands, _____ of the land is below sea level.
2. In 1953, a storm surge caused the water to rise to _____ meters above sea level.
3. The Delta Works system will withstand the type of storm that only occurs once in every _____ years.
4. The Delta Works sea barriers protect _____ kilometers of dikes on the estuaries.
5. A planning commission estimates that the Netherlands may see a rise in the North Sea of _____ meters by 2100.
6. It is a fact that that _____ of the world's _____ largest cities are on flood plains.

About you

D **Answer the questions with your own opinions.**

1. What was the most interesting thing you learned about the Delta Works in the Netherlands?

_____

2. Do you think other countries will invest in projects like the Delta Works? Why or why not?

_____

Current events

Lesson A Vocabulary News analysis

A Complete the article with the correct forms of the verbs in the box. There are two extra verbs.

clear	compensate	escalate	make	mobilize	plan	plunge

TOP STORIES	NATIONAL	WORLD	BUSINESS	ENTERTAINMENT

Looking back at the challenges the president faced in his first term

The president certainly had his work cut out for him during his first 100 days. Just before he came into office, the stock market _____[1] to a record low, resulting in job losses and economic stress for the country. The economy has since _____[2] a modest recovery, but the country is still facing financial difficulties. The initial downturn prompted widespread protests against corrupt banking and corporate practices. The demonstrators were furious that banks refused to _____[3] victims who had no control over how the banks handled their money. The president was actively involved in pushing for new legislation to mitigate these problems in the future. That did not stop the protests, however, and eventually authorities had to _____[4] riot squads as tensions _____[5] .

B Rewrite the bold parts of the sentences with expressions made up of words from each box. Write the verbs in the correct forms.

announce	cause	consider	contain	fuel	go	rule out	undergo

his campaign	off	speculation	the possibility
legal action	routine surgery	the explosion	the spill

Six months later, the president was faced with another challenge. A bomb **exploded** _____[1] in front of two government offices, causing extensive loss of life. The investigation into who or what **was behind the blast** _____[2] continues, and the president has not publicly **said it is not possible** _____[3] that terrorists were behind the attack. Just as the nation emerged from that crisis, the country's worst ever oil spill occurred off the East Coast. It took weeks before the company responsible could **hold back the oil leaking** _____[4], forcing the president to declare the area a national disaster. Damages have so far run into billions of dollars, and thousands of affected businesses are known to be **thinking about suing** _____[5]. Finally, the president's sudden hospitalization a few months before the end of his term **encouraged people to wonder** _____[6] that he would not run again. However, two days later, his press secretary confirmed that he was simply **having a simple operation** _____[7], and a week later the president officially **said that he would run** _____[8] his campaign for re-election.

Lesson A Grammar Reporting events in progress

A Circle the best options to complete the news brief.

NEWS BRIEF

An end to the fighting?

After months of bitter struggle, the tide now seems to **have been turning / be turning** in the civil war. Over the last few weeks, opposition forces appear to **have been regaining / be regaining** the ground they lost last winter. Furthermore, international peace brokers were said to **have been reaching / be reaching** a critical point in peace negotiations. Since arriving in New York on Sunday, representatives from all parties are said to **be negotiating / have been negotiating** a ceasefire agreement. Political analysts believe that prior to the talks, the president **may be holding out / may have been holding out** for outside military assistance, but he is now rumored to **be considering / have been considering** a power-sharing agreement with the opposition.

B Complete the news brief with continuous infinitive forms of the verbs given.

Possible student tuition increases

Thousands of students were said _____[1] (prepare) for bad news ahead of an expected announcement of an increase in tuition fees. University officials and a representative board of students will _____[2] (discuss) this divisive issue for two days by midnight tonight, which is the agreed deadline for an agreement. Despite some early signs of an agreement, hopes of reaching a compromise now appear _____[3] (fade). Student leaders have warned that students would _____[4] (take) action. Sara Folly, a political science major, had this to say: "I decided to skip classes and show my support to the board of students. The university authorities seem _____[5] (not listen) to us. Free education is something I really believe in." Tensions in college towns are said _____[6] (increase) since the start of the tuition discussions, and police are said _____[7] (monitor) the situation closely.

C Rewrite the underlined verbs. Add the verbs given and use continuous infinitive forms. Sometimes there is more than one possible answer.

1. The president's health problems <u>are hindering</u> his re-election campaign. (say)

   _____

2. Hopes of a lasting peace <u>have grown</u> since the ceasefire agreement. (appear)

   _____

3. The public prosecutor <u>is considering</u> legal action against corrupt banking CEOs later this year. (think)

   _____

4. Sporting officials say that the games <u>have gone</u> smoothly so far. (seem)

   _____

About you

D Write your own news report about a current event or situation that is causing concern.

_____

_____

Lesson B Grammar Describing what should happen

A Read the journalism professor's comments. Then complete the textbook sentences that reflect those views. Use the subjunctive form of the bold verbs.

1. *"The mainstream news industry depends on journalism **maintaining** industry expectations."*
   It is important that the established press _____ professional standards.

2. *"If certain editorial processes **are applied**, then quality journalism is possible."*
   It is essential that certain editorial processes _____ to ensure quality journalism.

3. *First of all, a journalist needs **to consult** different sources to have sufficient background for a story."*
   It is crucial that the journalist _____ various sources to establish the full context of a news item.

4. *Before submitting the story to the editor, he or she must **check** that all the facts are accurate."*
   Before the story is filed, it is essential that he or she _____ all the facts carefully.

5. *You can lose readers if there **are** spelling and grammar mistakes, so any errors need to be **corrected** by a proofreader."*
   Readers demand that spelling and grammar _____ correct. Therefore, it is essential that a proofreader _____ errors before publication.

6. *"News providers lose business if stories **are published** late. Some have to show that they **are** the very first with breaking news."*
   It is necessary that stories _____ as quickly as possible. There is a requirement on some organizations that they _____ the first ones to publish breaking news.

B Circle the best options to complete the sentences.

1. Many viewers have said that a recent political documentary _____ accurate and objective.
   a. be   b. was   c. seem
2. To maintain press standards, it's crucial that any news item _____ completely error free.
   a. are   b. reads   c. be
3. The judge requested that the media _____ the victim's identity.
   a. not reveal   b. not revealing   c. not be revealed
4. The paper's insistence that the reporter _____ her sources was in line with reporting ethics.
   a. conceal   b. concealing   c. be concealed
5. It's possible for anyone _____ breaking news via smartphones and social media.
   a. be published   b. publish   c. to publish
6. Editors demand that their publication's reputation _____ by poor journalistic standards.
   a. be not harmed   b. not be harmed   c. are not harmed

About you

C Answer the questions with your own opinions.

1. Do you use a news source that you trust more than others? If so, what is it?

   _____

   _____

2. What makes some news sources more trustworthy than others?

   _____

   _____

Lesson C Conversation strategies

A Complete the conversation with the expressions in the box. Write the letters a–i. There are three extra expressions.

a. choosing your style	f. supermarkets, newsstands, even pharmacies
b. most tabloids	g. the content
c. my colleagues	h. the reporter
d. reading rumors and looking at celebrities	i. your choice
e. seeing them everywhere	

Zoe Have you noticed how many people read tabloids? Like, _____¹, they buy them all the time. I mean, _____², I don't know why they want to do that.

Chan-Sook I know. They're all about gossip and sensation. There seems to be a huge market for that kind of thing.

Zoe I know. And I mean, _____³, they all sell them. You can't avoid them. It's so annoying, _____⁴.

Chan-Sook Yeah, and, _____⁵ of most of them, it's not really news, is it?

Zoe What gets me is all the bad news. I mean, _____⁶, they're full of people's misfortunes.

Chan-Sook Yeah, well, bad news sells, I guess. You don't buy a tabloid newspaper to feel good about the world!

B Complete the conversation with *this, that, these,* or *those.*

A Hey. Did I tell you? There's _____¹ new tenant in my apartment block. And you won't believe who it is.

B Let me guess. It's one of _____² crazy celebrities from the tabloids.

A Good guess, but not quite. You know _____³ anchor for the morning news on Channel 2?

B _____⁴ handsome guy who wears bowties? Is it him?

A Uh-huh. We keep meeting on the stairs and having _____⁵ really interesting conversations.

B That's amazing. He's smart. You know, how he asks _____⁶ difficult questions in interviews.

A Yeah, and you know how he also has _____⁷ quirky sense of humor on TV? Well, he does in real life, too. He's quite a character.

About you

C Complete the comments with information that is true for you. Then, explain your answer. Think of how to highlight the topics you are talking about. Try to use *this, these, that,* and *those* in your answers.

1. _____ , they don't really appeal to me. I don't know why people watch that stuff. I mean,

_____

_____

_____

2. It's _____ , being able to get in-depth coverage of events at the click of a button.
   On the other hand, _____

_____

_____

Lesson D   Reading   Newspapers

A   Prepare Why do you think the newspaper market has been declining? Check (✔) the reasons.

1. ☐ The entertainment industry has become more popular than news. _____
2. ☐ Radio has taken part of the newspaper market. _____
3. ☐ The quality of journalism has declined. _____
4. ☐ People are reluctant to pay for news. _____

B   Read for main ideas Read the article. Does the author mention any of the reasons in Exercise A? Write Y (yes) or N (no).

Why are newspapers dying?

The future of print journalism remains unclear

1 For people in the news business, it's hard to avoid the sense that newspapers are at death's door. Every day brings news of layoffs, bankruptcies, and closings in the print journalism industry.

2 But why are things so dire at the moment?

The decline begins with radio and TV

3 Newspapers have a history that dates back centuries. And while their roots are in the 1600s, newspapers thrived in the U.S. well into the twentieth century.

4 But with the advent of radio and later TV, newspaper circulation (the number of copies sold) began a gradual but steady decline. By the mid-twentieth century, people didn't have to rely on newspapers as their sole source of news. That was especially true of breaking news, which could be conveyed more quickly via broadcast media.

5 And as television newscasts became more sophisticated, TV became the dominant mass medium. This trend accelerated with the rise of CNN and 24-hour cable news networks.

Newspapers begin to disappear

6 Afternoon newspapers were the first casualties. People coming home from work began turning on the TV instead of opening a newspaper, and afternoon papers in the 1950s and 1960s saw circulations plunge and profits dry up. TV also increasingly captured more of the ad revenue that newspapers had relied on.

7 But even with TV grabbing more audience and ad dollars, newspapers managed to survive. Papers couldn't compete in terms of speed, but they could provide the in-depth news coverage that TV news never could.

8 So savvy editors retooled papers with this in mind. More stories were written with a feature-type approach that emphasized storytelling over breaking news, and papers were redesigned to be more visually appealing, with emphasis on clean layouts and graphic design.

The emergence of the Internet

9 But if TV represented a body blow to the newspaper industry, the World Wide Web may be the nail in the coffin. With the emergence of the Internet in the 1990s, vast amounts of information were suddenly free for the taking. Most newspapers, not wanting to be left behind, started websites in which they essentially gave away their most valuable commodity – their content – for free. This model continues to be predominant today.

10 Now, many analysts believe this was possibly a fatal mistake. Many once-loyal newspaper readers realized that if they could conveniently access news online for free, there was little reason to pay for a newspaper subscription.

The recession worsens print journalism's woes

11 Recent economic hard times have accelerated the problem. Revenue from print ads has plunged, and even online ad revenue, which publishers hoped would make up the difference, has slowed. And websites like Craigslist have eaten away at classified ad revenue.

12 "The online business model just won't support newspapers at the level Wall Street demands," says Chip Scanlan of The Poynter Institute, a journalism think tank. "Craigslist has decimated newspaper classifieds."

13 With profits plunging, newspaper publishers have responded with layoffs and cutbacks, but Scanlan worries this will make things worse.

14 "They're not helping themselves by whacking sections and laying people off," he says. "They're cutting the things that people look for in newspapers."

15 Indeed, that's the conundrum facing newspapers and their readers. All agree that newspapers still represent an unrivaled source of in-depth news, analysis, and opinion, and that if papers disappear, there will be nothing to take their place.

What the future holds

16 Opinions abound as to how newspapers can survive. Many say papers must charge for their web content in order to support print issues. Others say printed papers will soon go the way of the Studebaker* and that newspapers are destined to become online-only entities.

17 But what actually happens remains anybody's guess.

*Studebaker—an automobile manufacturer in the United States that ultimately went out of business in the 1960s.

SOURCE: journalism.about.com

C Understanding viewpoints **Check (✔) the points that the writer makes in the article.**

☐ 1. The newspaper industry has always struggled in the U.S.

☐ 2. Twenty-four-hour cable news networks helped to make TV news dominate.

☐ 3. Afternoon papers were the first type of newspaper to disappear.

☐ 4. TV news tended to provide more in-depth coverage than newspapers.

☐ 5. Savvy editors launched new advertising and marketing campaigns to save their newspapers.

☐ 6. The decline in newspaper circulation began with the popularization of the Internet.

☐ 7. Profits from newspaper advertisements have been decreasing.

☐ 8. Laying off workers and making cutbacks is the only way forward if newspapers want to survive.

☐ 9. Other forms of media can't compete with newspapers when it comes to analysis and opinion.

☐ 10. There's a strong chance that free Internet content will bring about the end of print newspapers.

D Read for main ideas **Circle the correct information to make true sentences about the article.**

1. The history of newspapers began in the **seventeenth / twentieth** century.

2. In the middle of the twentieth century, sales of newspapers began to decrease **rapidly / slowly**.

3. To compete with TV, newspaper stories focused on **breaking news / detailed news coverage**.

4. Many experts think it was an error for newspapers to **go online and start websites / charge only for print**.

5. The conundrum facing newspapers today is that they are cutting back on what people **want / don't want** from them.

6. Some people believe that like the Studebaker, printed papers will become **a thing of the past / more expensive**.

E Read for detail **Are the sentences true or false, or is the information not given? Write T, F, or NG. Correct the false sentences.**

1. The newspaper industry has a long and largely prosperous history. _____

2. Newspaper workforces have lately been shrinking. _____

3. By 1950, TV advertising revenue had doubled. _____

4. To try and win back readers, newspapers changed the look of the page. _____

5. Most big newspapers have recently started charging subscriptions for online content. _____

6. Wall Street investors are hoping that online news will save the newspaper industry. _____

7. Craigslist is a more popular classified ads source than both print and online newspapers. _____

8. It is clear what the future holds for newspapers. _____

F **Imagine that you work as a consultant in the news industry. A news corporation has asked**

About you **you for advice on how to encourage younger readers to buy their print newspaper. Write your advice.**

_____

_____

_____

_____

Writing Writing a summary

A Read the summary of the article *Why are newspapers dying?* Circle the correct verbs.

According to the article, *Why are newspapers dying?*, the advent of TV and radio, amongst other things, **is / are** to blame for the decline of newspapers. By the mid-twentieth century, most people considered that breaking news **was / were** presented more efficiently by these new media, and this appealed to advertisers, resulting in a loss of revenue for newspapers. Since the rise of the Internet, free content **has / have** become the predominant online news model — a strategic error which unfortunately **has / have** lost newspapers millions in potential revenue. Finally, a number of recent developments **is / are** adding to newspapers' woes. Print and online newspaper classifieds **struggle / struggles** to compete with Craigslist, and the economic downturn of recent times **has / have** forced papers to cut content and lay people off. The author of the article **concludes / conclude** by wondering whether charging for online papers could subsidize the print versions or whether print papers will disappear completely.

B Complete the sentences with a correct form of the verbs given.

1. The revenue potential of the news websites _____ not clearly understood when the Internet first emerged. (be)
2. In line with the trend at that time, online news _____ provided free of charge. (be)
3. Today, the number of news providers with an Internet presence _____ to include small, local papers. (grow)
4. People now _____ to be able to download their news for free, and this has affected sales of print papers. (expect)
5. A number of newspapers now _____ for online access, and readers who are used to free content _____ to make a decision. (charge / need)
6. Quality reporting and free access _____ available elsewhere. Therefore, do readers jump ship, or stay loyal to their original news provider? (be)

C Editing Correct the sentences. There may be more than one error in each one.

1. The number of blogs that analyzes the news have grown during the past five years.
2. The amount of spam that arrives in my inbox seem to be increasing.
3. The most exciting opportunities for someone who has been trained as a reporter is in online news.
4. The quality of news reporting that are available online are not always consistent.
5. The use of microblogs that is read by most young people have dramatically changed news reporting.
6. Satirical news and stories which appears on some websites are often believed to be true.

D Write a summary of an interesting news story. Be sure to follow the guidelines for summary writing. Then check your summary for errors.

Listening extra Journalism debate

A Read the expressions in the box, which are from a debate about journalism. What do they mean? Write the letters a–f.

1. a whistle blower _____
2. hack into (voicemail) _____
3. a code of ethics _____
4. a tabloid _____
5. a regulation _____
6. wrongdoing _____

a. behaving badly or illegally
b. an official rule
c. someone who reveals illegal activities in a workplace
d. a set of moral rules
e. a popular type of newspaper
f. access illegally

B ⬇ What do you think the topic of the debate will be? Write an idea. Then listen and check your guess.

My guess _____   The topic is _____

C ⬇ Listen again. Circle the best option to complete the sentences.

1. Dr. Gilmore thinks it is _____ for journalists to hack into email and other accounts.
   a. unethical   b. unavoidable   c. natural
2. He thinks that journalists need to _____ .
   a. be more careful   b. regain public support   c. regulate themselves
3. Marion McCall thinks the result of rules and regulations in journalism may mean _____ .
   a. greater social change   b. better reporting   c. wrongdoing won't be reported
4. She thinks unethical behavior by journalists is _____ .
   a. acceptable   b. unprofessional   c. widespread
5. Dr. Gilmore believes that the public has a right _____ .
   a. to privacy   b. to newspaper records   c. to see corruption exposed
6. Marion McCall believes that regulations should not prevent journalists from _____ .
   a. saving lives   b. engaging in illegal activity   c. making bad decisions

D ⬇ Listen again. Complete the sentences with no more than four words.

1. We should be demanding that journalists _____ email accounts.
2. Cases like the jailed journalists have had negative consequences for the _____ .
3. Clearly, it's every journalist's responsibility to _____ .
4. It's important that one consider the _____ of a story, not just how it was researched.
5. A journalist might go into a social network or email account for information that _____ .
6. There are always exceptional cases where journalists have to _____ .

About you **E** Answer the questions with your own opinions.

1. Which speaker did you think was more convincing? Why?

   _____

2. Which information presented in the debate would you like to know more about? Why?

   _____

3. Think of an example of an ethical dilemma that a journalist might face.

   _____

> Now complete the *Unit 10 Progress chart* on page 101.

Unit 11 Is it real?

Lesson A Grammar Talking about the future

A Complete the blog post with correct forms of the *be to* expressions and the verbs given.

HOME
ABOUT ME
BLOG ARCHIVE
CONTACT

According to the weather report, another tropical cyclone _____¹ (be / strike) the southern U.S. coast this week, severe floods _____² (be about / hit) Western Europe, and the heat wave plaguing Australia _____³ (be set / continue). Perhaps, like me, you're wondering if all the damage and destruction from floods, tornadoes, and earthquakes _____⁴ (be set / occur) regularly across the globe. I did some research, and as far as I can tell, most experts attribute our changing weather patterns to global warming. Some of them say it _____⁵ (be bound / happen) sooner or later because our climate _____⁶ (be set / change) naturally every few million years. Perhaps that's true, but if the environmentalists are correct, climate change and natural disasters _____⁷ (be actually set / intensify) because of all the junk we put into the atmosphere. Hmm . . . so what kind of weird weather _____⁸ (be about / hit) your area? Personally, I think it's time to go green.

B Complete the sentences with correct forms of the *be to* expressions given.

1. If extraterrestrials exist, what would happen if they _____ (be) turn their attention to our planet? Doomsayers regularly claim that aliens _____ (be bound) invade Earth, and we humans will have to defend our planet!

2. How much importance can one attach to the sixteenth-century writings of Nostradamus? If you believe his followers, he predicted that France _____ (be) undergo a revolution in the 1790s. Fortunately, his prediction that civilization _____ (be) come to an end in 2012 has been proven wrong!

3. Some scientists say our grandchildren _____ (be bound) experience severe food shortages if the population _____ (be) continue growing at current rates. They estimate that humanity must shrink two-thirds by mid-century if we _____ (be) avoid spiraling food prices and massive starvation.

About you

C. Answer the questions with information that is true for you.

1. What events are about to happen in your city or town?

_____

_____

2. What is the weather in your area likely and not likely to do at this time of year?

_____

_____

3. What kinds of challenges are the people in your country bound to experience in the next few months?

_____

_____

Lesson B Vocabulary Idioms and phrasal verbs with *turn*

A Match the words in bold with the expressions in the box that have a similar meaning.
Write the letters a–f. There is one extra expression.

a. turn a blind eye (to something)
b. turn down
c. turn out
d. turn (something) around
e. turn to
f. turning point

1. It's sometimes hard for people to **change** their lives **in a positive way** after they have gotten a criminal record. _____
2. There are some opportunities you have to **decline** in life. Not all of them are good. _____
3. Every person has a positive quality — sometimes you just have to **ignore** people's weaknesses. _____
4. Life can be difficult for young people if they don't have role models to **approach** for advice. _____
5. Most people can identify a **significant event** that really changed their lives. _____

B Complete the conversation with correct forms of the *turn* expressions in the box.

turn back the clock	turn out	turning point	turn (your) back on
turn into	turn over a new leaf	turn (something) around	

A You remember Jeff Kline, the big guy who used to frighten people in high school? He just called me to apologize, 20 years later!

B Jeff Kline? Wow, I can't believe it! So, has he _____[1] a nice person?

A Well, he was very apologetic. He said he knew he couldn't _____[2] , but he wished he had behaved better all those years ago. And I know people who really like him now. They say he's _____[3] .

B That couldn't have been easy — he had a difficult time when he was a kid. I remember he was always getting in trouble.

A Apparently, the _____[4] was when he met his wife. She helped him _____ his _____[5] all of that.

B That's a nice story. And I'm glad things _____[6] OK for Jeff. You have to admire people who _____ their lives _____[7] .

About you

C Use six of the *turn* expressions in the lesson to write sentences that have meaning for you.

1. _____ .
2. _____ .
3. _____ .
4. _____ .
5. _____ .
6. _____ .

Lesson B   Grammar   Information focus

A **Complete the blog post with passive or active forms of the verbs given.**

Home About Me Past Blogs Contact Me

Are you someone who deserves _____[1] (recognize) for staying true to your dreams? I'd like _____[2] (place) in that category, but I've become more boring and conventional than I originally planned! For the last year or so, my mind appears _____[3] (take over) by mortgage payments and other financial worries. Not only that, but life has gotten so busy and I can't avoid _____[4] (catch up) in meetings and traffic jams. I have a friend, though, who seems _____[5] (achieve) the life he always wanted. Nobody could ever _____[6] (persuade) him that to a nine-to-five job was the way to go. No, sir! He'd rather _____[7] (leave) alone in his beach cabin, to write, surf, and breathe in the fresh air. He says it's not worth _____[8] (make) miserable by a regular job. He's just signed a lucrative book deal, and for that he really deserves _____[9]. (respect) He's made it and he's avoided _____[10] (force) to postpone the good life. How many people can say that?

B **Rewrite the sentences using a passive form of the underlined verbs. Start with the words given. Sometimes there is more than one correct answer.**

1. I want people to <u>remember</u> me for the charity work I do in the community.
   I'd like *to be remembered for the charity work I do in the community.* .

2. My grandmother <u>taught</u> me to appreciate the funny side of life.
   I remember _____ .

3. My English teacher <u>has</u> unfairly <u>labeled</u> me the class clown.
   I don't think I deserve _____ .

4. I wouldn't <u>allow</u> sensitive viewers to watch a movie about me!
   Sensitive viewers shouldn't _____ .

5. My mother <u>gave</u> me all my sister's old clothes to wear, which I always hated.
   I didn't enjoy _____ .

6. I wouldn't want scriptwriters to <u>portray</u> my life dishonestly.
   I wouldn't want my life _____ .

7. My college <u>offered</u> me a graduate school scholarship.
   I didn't expect _____ .

About you

C **Unscramble the questions. Then write answers that are true for you.**

1. do you / What / be / to / appreciated for? / want / qualities
   Q: _____   A: _____

2. kind of career advice / given / What / be / today? / should / to young people
   Q: _____   A: _____

3. of your / you want / How / would / to be / life? / in a movie / portrayed
   Q: _____   A: _____

Lesson C Conversation strategies

A **Complete the conversations with the expressions in the box.**

be too happy about	doesn't sit right with me	that's not good
doesn't seem right	I'm not comfortable with	that would be my concern

1. *A* I have a friend who does a lot of online dating. But his profile isn't accurate. That just
   _____ to me.
   B Well, I think it's OK to emphasize the best parts of your personality, but
   _____ people who lie about things like their job or their age.
   A My friend wrote that he works in the theater, but he just has a cleaning job there. And his
   profile picture is about 10 years old!
   B If it were me, I wouldn't _____ that. I assume he's still looking.
   A Well, yeah, he is.

2. *A* My friend Sue asked me over to her new house, but I said I was busy again, which isn't
   actually true. I know _____ , but I just couldn't face an hour in
   traffic.
   B It's too bad you don't see each other much now that she's moved. You'll end up losing touch.
   Well, _____ .
   A Yeah. The problem is, neither of us likes driving in traffic.
   B Gosh. It _____ that something like that can get in the way of a
   good friendship.

B **Rewrite the responses with *to me, to some people,* etc.**

1. *A* You know what gets me? When people say they're going to get back to you about something,
   and they don't.
   B Yeah. ~~I think~~ To me that's rude, but some people think that's perfectly fine.

2. *A* I still haven't been paid for some work I did for a software company last month. Every time I
   call, they say my check's in the mail.

   B I don't think that's right. They probably think it's normal.

3. *A* One of my friends is always late. She calls to say she's on her way, but I know she isn't.

   B Yeah, no. What else does she lie about? I think that's also an issue.

About you **C** **Circle the correct options to complete the conversations. Sometimes both are correct.
Then write your own responses to A giving your opinions.**

1. *A* My friend asked me out on date, but I don't feel that way about him. I can't tell him that,
   though. **That's my concern / To me**, that would be too insensitive.
   B But if you don't say something, he might think you're interested. **That's my concern / To me.**

   _____

2. *A* My roommate gave me some of her stories to read, and they're terrible! I suppose I could tell
   her they're great, but **that doesn't seem right / I'm not comfortable with that**. I mean, she's
   hoping to be a writer one day.
   B No, **that doesn't sit right / that's not good**, either. **To me / I'm not happy about**, it seems like
   she needs some constructive criticism. I'm sure she'll appreciate that.

   _____

Lesson D Reading Second Mona Lisa

A Prepare The words in the box are from an article about a painting. Use the words to predict what the article is about. Write down your ideas.

art collector	earlier version	similarities and differences	the Mona Lisa
authenticity	Leonardo da Vinci	speculate	well-made copy

B Read for main ideas Read the article. Were any of your predictions about the article correct?

Second Mona Lisa unveiled for first time in 40 years

1 It's a mystery straight out of the *Da Vinci Code*. A famous portrait, hidden away in a Swiss bank vault for 40 years, with the potential to break open a mystery more than 500 years old. A second, earlier version of the *Mona Lisa* was unveiled to the public today, a version that experts say they can prove is the work of the master himself.

2 Known as the *Isleworth Mona Lisa*, the painting was discovered shortly before World War I by English art collector Hugh Blaker, who purchased it from the noble family to which it had previously belonged. Blaker then moved the painting to his studio in Isleworth, England, giving it its iconic name.

3 During WWI, the painting was moved to America for safekeeping. The portrait eventually made its way back to Europe, where it was analyzed in Italy before being sent to the Swiss bank vault for safekeeping. Since that time, experts from the non-profit Mona Lisa Foundation have been working to prove or disprove the portrait's authenticity.

4 "When we do a very elementary mathematical test, we have discovered that all of the elements of the two bodies – the two people, the two sitters – are in exactly the same place," art historian and foundation member Stanley Feldman told The Associated Press.

5 "It strikes us that in order for that to be so accurate, so meticulously exact, only the person who did one did the other. … It's an extraordinary revelation in itself, and we think it's valid."

6 Such similarities aside, the two *Mona Lisa*'s have many notable differences, the Isleworth version is larger and features columns on either side of the figure, believed to be Lisa del Giocondo. The version that hangs in Paris' Louvre Museum is narrower and features no such columns.

Isleworth Mona Lisa

7 The Isleworth painting was done on canvas, while the Louvre painting, which features a far more detailed background, was done on wood. The woman in the Isleworth version also appears younger than she does in the Louvre, leading to the theory that the portrait might have been painted earlier, consequently featuring a younger del Giocondo.

8 The foundation's claims aside, many in the art and scientific community remain unconvinced.

9 "It's a perfectly honest, well-made early copy," Martin Kemp, an Oxford University professor and da Vinci expert, told ABC News today. "Pictures were copied [because] you couldn't go to the Internet and order a reproduction. So if you wanted something like that [the *Mona Lisa*] and you couldn't get a hold of a Leonardo, you would order a copy."

10 With the debate still raging, it is difficult to reach a definite conclusion about the painting's authenticity. So, until the foundation releases more evidence, it looks as though experts will be left to speculate about whether the *Isleworth Mona Lisa* is the work of the Renaissance man himself, or one very gifted impressionist.

SOURCE: ABC News

C Read for detail **Are the sentences true or false, or is the information not given in the article? Write T, F, or NG. Correct the false sentences.**

1. A second, earlier version of the *Mona Lisa* was secretly kept in a Swiss bank for 40 years. _____

2. Hugh Blaker believed in the authenticity of the painting he bought. _____

3. The portrait was sent from Europe to America because at the time it was thought that America was a safer place. _____

4. During the twentieth century, the painting was kept in three different countries. _____

5. The fact that the women in the two paintings are in exactly the same position was discovered through a detailed scientific analysis. _____

6. The opinion of the Mona Lisa Foundation is that Leonardo da Vinci painted both versions of the *Mona Lisa.* _____

7. The total size of the two paintings is exactly the same. _____

8. Some people believe that the portraits feature the same woman painted at different times. _____

9. It's possible that Leonardo da Vinci made copies of his own and other people's paintings. _____

10. According to the article, in order to end the speculation about the *Isleworth Mona Lisa,* more experts need to analyze the evidence. _____

D Understanding reference **Find the sentences in the article. What do the underlined words refer to? Check the correct answer.**

1. It's a <u>mystery</u> straight out of the *Da Vinci Code.* (para. 1)
    a. determining who painted the second version of the *Mona Lisa*
    b. determining why the portrait was hidden in a Swiss bank vault

2. Since <u>that time</u> . . . (para. 3)
    a. WWI
    b. when the painting was sent to the Swiss bank vault

3. It strikes <u>us</u> . . . (para. 5)
    a. the people who work for the Mona Lisa Foundation
    b. the people who work for the Associated Press

4 . . . . in order for <u>that</u> to be so accurate . . . (para. 5)
    a. the fact that the two bodies are in the same place
    b. the fact that the parts of the two women are the same person.

5. . . . <u>who</u> did one did the other. (para. 5)
    a. the person who did the elementary mathematical test
    b. the painter of the *Mona Lisa* portraits

6 <u>Such similarities</u> aside (para. 6)
    a. the fact the sitters are in the same place
    b. the fact that the paintings are by the same artist.

7. . . . or <u>one very gifted impressionist.</u> (para. 10)
    a. an artist
    b. a fake painting

About you **E** React **Answer the questions with information that is true for you.**

1. Which facts in the article surprised you? Which ones didn't?

_____

_____

2. What new things about art did you learn from the article?

_____

_____

Writing An opinion essay

A Circle the best expressions to complete the essay.

The case for regulating the rhino horn industry

Rhino horn has been used in traditional medicines to treat fever, rheumatism, and other ailments for thousands of years. Demand is at an all-time high, mostly supplied by illegal rhino poaching, and **given / no matter** what conservation measures are put in place, more wild rhinos are being killed each year. Some animal activists question why the industry exists at all, **considering that / provided that** rhino horn is composed entirely of keratin (the chief component in hair and fingernails). **In view of the fact / Yet** others point out that rhino horn is a cultural icon, and people have the right to use it **regardless of / in light of** skeptics who deny its medicinal effectiveness. Fortunately, there is a way to preserve rhinos and supply the horn market at the same time. Like hair and nails, rhino horn grows back, **as long as / yet** it isn't entirely removed. So it can be farmed in captive breeding programs, a practice that already exists in China. Therefore, **in view of the fact / no matter** that certain subspecies could soon become extinct, it is my opinion that governments should issue rhino-farming licenses and regulate the rhino-horn industry.

B Complete the sentences with the expressions in the box. Sometimes more than one answer is possible.

given that	in light of	irrespective of	provided	regardless of	yet

1. The killing of rhinos can be stopped _____ the authorities are willing to regulate the rhino-horn market. The question is, will they?
2. The market for illegal products will continue to exist _____ government attempts to prohibit such industries.
3. Demand for rhino horn is set to grow _____ the recent rumor that powdered rhino horn can cure cancer.
4. Banning the trade in endangered species seems to push animals closer to extinction, _____ how severe the penalties are.
5. Businesses are often efficient at producing and protecting valuable species. _____ governments seem reluctant to involve them in conservation.
6. The trade in rhino horn should be legalized _____ it is possible to remove most of the horn without harming the animal.

C Editing Correct the sentences by replacing the underlined expressions with other conjunctions or adverbs from the lesson. Sometimes more than one answer is possible.

1. Some people think that the rhino horn ban can work <u>provided that</u> the ivory ban worked. However, the long-term success of the ivory ban remains questionable.
2. The illegal trade of animal body parts continues <u>assuming</u> the fact that many animal species are close to extinction.
3. There is a thriving, legal trade in farmed crocodile skin that has not affected wild crocodiles. <u>As long as</u> some people think a legal trade in rhino horn would endanger wild rhinos.
4. Endangered species can be saved <u>given that</u> governments explore ways to protect them.

D Write an essay giving your opinion about the market for endangered animal products. Use the academic conjunctions and adverbs from this lesson. Then check your essay for errors.

Listening extra Fake résumés

A Look at the list of things that some people have been known to falsify on résumés and job applications. Write three more things.

JOHN SMITH

Philadelphia, Pennsylvania
(555) 555-5555
John_Smith@cup.com

OBJECTIVE:

Be a productive team leader that moves the company forward

PROFESSIONAL EXPERIENCE:

VP of International Sales for Acme Soda, Inc.	2012-Current
National Sales Manager for Philly Soda, Inc.	2000-2012
District Sales Manager for Philly Soda, Inc.	1998-2000
Salesman for Philly Soda, Inc.	1996-1998

EDUCATION:

☐ current job title
☐ current salary
☐ date of birth
☐ education
☐ periods of unemployment
☐ reason for leaving a job
☐ references

_____

_____

_____

B ⬇ Listen to the interview about false information on résumés. Check (✔) the items above that the people talk about.

C ⬇ Listen again. Check (✔) the correct answers to the questions.

1. What are you likely to find on most résumés?
   ☐ a. exaggerations
   ☐ b. false job descriptions

2. How can managers prevent their companies from wasting time and money?
   ☐ a. by not interviewing suspicious candidates
   ☐ b. by doing phone interviews

3. What makes Sarah Lim become suspicious?
   ☐ a. job descriptions that don't match skills and experience
   ☐ b. unexplained periods of unemployment

4. What kind of fake education information do some candidates provide?
   ☐ a. They claim to have attended prestigious schools.
   ☐ b. They list degrees that they haven't actually completed.

5. What can suggest fake work experience?
   ☐ a. candidates listing companies with technical names
   ☐ b. candidates listing companies with unusual addresses

6. How does Sarah Lim check salary information?
   ☐ a. She asks applicants to provide their last tax return.
   ☐ b. She asks applicants to provide their last paycheck.

7. What warning does she give about references?
   ☐ a. Some candidates list relatives as references.
   ☐ b. Some candidates write their own references.

About you

D What do you think about putting false information on a résumé? Complete the sentences with your own views.

1. To me _____ .
2. I'm not comfortable with _____ .
3. _____ . That would be my concern.

Now complete the *Unit 11 Progress chart* on page 101.

12 Psychology

Lesson A Grammar Complex situations and events

A Put the words in bold into the correct order to complete the sentences in the email.

I drove up to New York to visit my mom last weekend. I was kind of tired, but I knew **me /
relaxing / to / wouldn't / she / kindly / take** _____[1] in front
of the TV. As I expected, **on / she / insisted / us / going** _____[2] to see
a Broadway show, followed by a meal at a fancy restaurant! It was fun, although **enjoy / didn't /
driving / I / her** _____[3] through several red lights on the way to the
theater. I hadn't realized how much her eyesight had deteriorated, and I had to express **about /
causing / my / concerns / her** _____[4] a serious accident. It was quite
a difficult moment, actually. **her / looking / I / remember** _____[5]
straight ahead and not saying anything. For the first time, **with / we / were / getting / her /
dealing** _____[6] old and the implications of that for the two of us.

B Read the rest of the email. Rewrite the bold parts of the sentences with an object and
an *-ing* form.

I think the driving situation allowed my mom to talk candidly about things. She said she
didn't like the fact that I lived _____*didn't like me living*_____[1] so far away. Also, she
didn't trust accountants, and she wasn't **comfortable with the fact that they handled**
_____[2] her finances. She wanted us to live closer, and she wanted
me to look after her accounts from now on. I guess this was bound to happen at some point,
but it was still a shock. My mother's always been a big **believer in the idea that people
should be** _____[3] independent, and I **recall that she always said**
_____[4] that I should always think for myself. I hate to **insist that she
should give up the car** _____[5], but I guess we're moving onto a new
stage in life, where I have to guide her.

About you

C Complete the sentences to make them true for you. Use an *-ing* form and any other
information.

1. When I was growing up, I remember my mother _____
   _____ .

2. In my opinion, parents should always insist on their children _____
   _____ .

3. I'm a great believer in people _____
   _____ .

Lesson B Vocabulary Phrasal verbs

A **Circle the correct phrasal verbs to complete the anecdote.**

Beware of con artists on classified ad websites! I learned that last summer when I used the Internet to look for a new apartment. The price of the one I **picked out / picked up on** — a renovated loft — seemed very reasonable, if the upscale neighborhood was anything to **give away / go by**. However, that didn't strike me as suspicious and I rushed to put down a deposit. A few days later, the ad was still up, listing the apartment as "available." I really should have **talked into / picked up on** the scam at that point, but I **was taken in by / played down** the "agent's" explanation. He said he'd forgotten his password to the website so he couldn't take the ad down. What finally **gave the game away / went by** was someone arriving to view the apartment while I was measuring it for new furniture! Of course, by then the agent had disappeared with the deposits of several naive "tenants." I guess it **comes down to / went about** the old saying: If it seems too good to be true, it probably is!

B **Complete each sentence with a verb (in the correct form) from box A and a word from box B.**

A				
give	go	play	put	talk

B				
about	away	behind	down	into

1. My boyfriend started seeing someone else! What _____ him _____ was her photo in his wallet.
2. I'm always wary of people who try to _____ you _____ quick moneymaking schemes.
3. Dreaming up ways to scam people isn't the best way to _____ _____ earning a living.
4. If you get a raw deal, you just have to _____ it _____ you and carry on with your life.
5. In interviews, company CEOs often _____ _____ poor results and focus on the future.

About you

C **Answer the questions with information that is true for you.**

1. Do you know anyone who is easily talked into things? Explain.

   _____

   _____

2. Some difficult situations are easier to put behind you than others. Give your opinion.

   _____

   _____

3. Think of an example where a lot of people were taken in by someone or something.

   _____

   _____

Lesson B Grammar Referring to people and things

A Complete the article on identity theft with appropriate pronouns. Sometimes there is more than one correct answer.

Identity theft on social networking sites

We like to keep in touch with _____¹ on social networking sites, but are we protecting _____² against the dangers of identity theft? An online "poser" could be using your photos and other information to set up a fake profile and then presenting _____³ or _____⁴ to others as you. In such a situation, "you" may unwittingly find _____⁵ spreading stories over the Internet, which seem believable because they include plausible information about your friends.

It's been widely reported how posers take people in by setting up celebrity profiles. They and their excited, naive fans then share personal information with _____⁶. Unfortunately, if you find _____⁷ in this compromised situation, you may discover that things like driver's licenses and even credit cards are being issued in your name.

Sometimes your social network _____⁸ isn't secure enough. So how does one go about safeguarding _____⁹ against posers? People create risks by posting photos that are downloadable, and by sharing sensitive details about _____¹⁰, like their address and date of birth. To be on the safe side, make sure that your social networking profile can only be accessed by trusted friends.

B Complete the sentences with appropriate pronouns. Sometimes there is more than one correct answer.

1. I found my favorite actor on a social networking site and we "friended" _____ .
2. I fooled _____ into believing that he was the real actor and not a poser.
3. Certain things should have given him away, like when he described _____ as shy and lonely.
4. We chatted with _____ for a few months, and he talked me into sharing a lot of personal information.
5. Eventually my sister, who is one of my social networking contacts, became suspicious and decided to investigate him _____ .
6. She had picked up on the fact that we found _____ being contacted by people we don't often communicate with.
7. A trail of clues led to a poser representing _____ or herself as me on a different social networking site.
8. The site deleted the profile, but in the end, it comes down to you _____ being careful about sharing personal information.
9. The experience _____ turned out to be a useful one. I've been able to tell a lot of people about it. Hopefully, they'll be more careful, too.

About you **C** How can we protect ourselves against identity theft? Give your opinion and include pronouns from the lesson in your answer.

_____

_____

_____

_____

Lesson C Conversation strategies

A **Complete the conversation. Write a or b.**

Kasia Pete keeps getting turned down for a rental apartment. He says it's because homeowners disapprove of his long hair.

Becky He might be right. I mean, I *like* his hair, and he'd be a good tenant. But at the same time, _____¹ .
a. his hair creates an impression, and this is a conservative town
b. he'd be very reliable

Kasia Maybe. But if you look at it from Pete's perspective, _____² .
a. he should get his hair cut
b. it's not fair to be judged on your appearance

Becky Yes, but homeowners don't want to take risks. And by the same token, tenants should _____³ .
a. realize that the more conservative they look, the better their chances of securing an apartment
b. be able to wear scruffy clothes if they like

Kasia Well, I can see it from both sides. I accept that homeowners don't want to take risks. _____⁴ .
a. They're being unreasonable
b. But they could check his references to find out what kind of person he really is

B **Complete the conversations. Write the letters a–d. There is one extra answer.**

1. *A* My friend Sue's a really good server. She gets lots of tips.
   B _____ . People like it when servers look nice.

2. *A* My manager says she wants us all to look very stylish. She says it's good for business.
   B _____ Not everybody has the money to buy expensive clothes.

3. *A* My boss asked me if I still felt motivated. She said she'd noticed I wasn't wearing any makeup.
   B _____ Your appearance doesn't reflect your performance.

a. She could have anticipated that, to put it simply.
b. Well, that's none of her business, to put it politely.
c. That's really asking a bit much of people, to put it mildly.
d. Well, to put it bluntly, it's because she always looks fabulous.

C **Circle the correct options to complete the conversations. Sometimes both are correct.**

1. *A* One of my colleagues got really mad today. She came to work wearing this long dress, and one of the guys made some silly joke about her wearing a nightgown. She didn't like it, **equally / to put it mildly**.
   B Oh dear. I guess **if you look at it from / by the same token** the guy's perspective, it was just a joke. But, **at the same time / equally**, he should know not to comment on a colleague's appearance like that. It's unprofessional **equally / to put it bluntly**.

2. *A* My friend disapproves of commercials that only have good-looking people in them, **but I can see it from both sides / by the same token**. Companies have a right to sell products in the way they feel is best, don't you think?
   B Yes, **by the same token / at the same time**, they should have a sense of social responsibility. To put it **mildly / bluntly** commercials do tend to encourage the shallow obsession with looks that so many people have today.

Lesson D Reading Gender stereotypes

A Prepare **Check (✔) the statements that you think are true. Then read the article. Which statements are true according to Dr. Eliot?**

☐ Girls are more social and emotional than boys.   ☐ Boys are more athletic than girls.

☐ Boys are more aggressive than girls.   ☐ Girls write better than boys.

☐ Girls are less competitive than boys.   ☐ Boys are better at reading maps than girls.

BOYS and GIRLS: not as different as we thought

1   For decades, psychologists and researchers have been telling us the same old thing — boys and girls are fundamentally different. Their brains are different, their childhood development is different, their perceptions of the world around them are different. It's the old nature versus nurture debate, with many parents unmistakably believing that nature is the primary force in a child's development and that all parents can do is hang on for the ride.

2   But a new book by Lise Eliot, PhD, suggests that many of these differences are what we, the adults, make of them. She's done the equivalent of a meta-analysis on the research foundation for gender differences between boys and girls, and put into a consumer-digestible format. The results are summarized in her new book, *Pink Brain, Blue Brain*. As *Newsweek* summarized:

3   How we perceive children — sociable or remote, physically bold or reticent — shapes how we treat them and therefore what experiences we give them. Since life leaves footprints on the very structure and function of the brain, these various experiences produce sex differences in adult behavior and brains — the result not of innate and inborn nature but of nurture.

4   The gist of her findings is that many of the differences that parents believe are innate or nature-led are not. Motor skills? The same. Ability to have deep emotional feelings? The same. Aggressiveness? The same. Why do we observe such differences in little boys and girls? Because parents often unconsciously reinforce the gender stereotypes within their children:

5   "Oh, little Sally can't run as quickly as little Bobby."

6   "Oh, Mikey is always so aggressive; Angela is an angel in comparison!"

7   "Since little Eric doesn't seem to express many emotions, he must not be as emotional as little Hannah, who has an outburst at the drop of a hat!"

8   Our children become a self-fulfilling prophecy — they turn into the kids we, by and large, imagine them to be. Parents don't usually do this consciously, of course. It is the stereotyped roles hammered into us at an early age, reinforced by consumerism and toy makers and commercials, and our own mothers and fathers. Boys are athletic and competitive, while girls are less so, and more social and emotional. These are stereotypes we imprint on our children; they are not naturally this way.

9   There are *some* differences the research supports with robust data. Dr. Eliot found that girls write better and more easily than most boys, and that boys have a better sense of spatial navigation than girls (like in reading a map).

10   What Dr. Eliot is saying isn't really new. We've known for years that infant brains are extremely malleable. But she's put it into simple language and has done a good job summarizing the vast body of research to really help put all of that data into some context. Her argument that small differences at birth become amplified over time as we all work to reinforce the gender stereotypes resonates.

11   Children must learn to stray from their comfort zones, with parents helping them try new things and explore new ways of expressing themselves that perhaps don't feel natural at first, but will often come with time. Boys, for instance, should be encouraged and reinforced for being able to express their feelings. The book not only goes into what few differences really exist, but also explains what parents can do to help encourage their kids to go outside of their comfort zones.

SOURCE: Psych Central

B Paraphrase **Write the number of the paragraph next to each description.**

1. Parents have long felt that they have no influence over the forces of nature that control their children. _____

2. What parents have believed to be innate differences between boys and girls was found to be reinforced by stereotypes, not biological. _____

3. Children become a product of what is expected of them. _____

4. There are ways to help children become better at the things that aren't stereotypical to their respective gender. _____

C Check your understanding **Complete the sentences. Write a, b, or c.**

1. There is an old view that boys and girls are different because _____ .
   a. their biological make up is different
   b. their experiences are different
   c. parents treat them differently

2. According to Dr. Eliot, there is _____ adult gender behavior and the experiences we had as children.
   a. no connection between
   b. a direct link between
   c. a lack of understanding about

3. Eliot claims the reason boys and girls behave differently is because parents _____ stereotyped behavior in children.
   a. deliberately reinforce
   b. unintentionally emphasize
   c. reluctantly encourage

4. Eliot describes how ideas like male athleticism and emotional females are reinforced by _____ .
   a. children's toys
   b. advertising
   c. both

5. The idea that girls are better at writing and boys are better at reading maps is _____
   a. untrue
   b. backed up by research
   c. possible, but not proven

6. The writer of the article respects Dr. Eliot's ability to _____ gender research.
   a. draw new conclusions from
   b. question existing
   c. present

7. Dr. Eliot's book explains strategies that parents can utilize to help their children _____ .
   a. become better at sports
   b. become better writers
   c. try new things

D Understanding inference **Check (✔) the statements that are suggested in the article.**

1. ☐ The idea that all gender differences are natural is old-fashioned.
2. ☐ Boys and girls perceive the world differently.
3. ☐ Most parents accept that nurture is as important as nature in a child's development.
4. ☐ Dr. Eliot's book has been written in a way that ordinary people will be able to understand.
5. ☐ Our life experiences can cause men to think like women and vice versa.
6. ☐ We force gender stereotypes onto young people.
7. ☐ Women become more interested in consumerism than boys because of gender stereotyping.
8. ☐ The book gives a balanced view of how nature and nurture influence our development.
9. ☐ Boys and girls rarely find any common interests until they grow up.

About you **E** React **Do you think the media and the choices we make as consumers reinforce gender stereotypes? Give reasons for your answer.**

_____

_____

Writing A statistical report

A Circle the correct options to complete the statistical report.

READING *for* PLEASURE
among American youth

Reading for pleasure among children is a practice that can significantly boost reading test scores. According to research on American schoolchildren by the Data Resource Center for Child and Adolescent Health, . . .

- 16 percent of children do not read at all. There are twice **more / as many** boys **as / than** girls in this category.
- 44 percent of children read for at least 30 minutes a day, and 24 percent read for 30 minutes to an hour. Boys are just as likely to be in the first group **as / than** girls, but girls are more likely **as / than** boys to be in the second.
- 16 percent of children read for more than an hour a day. There are roughly 1.5 times **as / as many** girls **as / than** boys in this group.

It is widely believed that reading regularly to preschool children encourages them to develop reading habits. A survey by the Federal Interagency Forum in Child and Family Statistics on the likelihood of preschool children being read to reveals that:

- children from poor families are nearly 25 percent less likely to be read to **as / than** children from average income families.
- the chances of children with college-educated mothers being read to are more than twice **as high as / higher** in many cases **as / than** children whose mothers didn't complete high school.

Sources: Data Resource Center for Child & Adolescent Health and Centers for Disease Control & Prevention

B Complete the comparisons in the sentences with the information in parentheses.

1. More wealth often means better health. Children from average income families are _____ to be in good health _____ children from poor families. (1.5 times / likely)
2. There are more boys than girls with Attention Deficit Disorder (ADD). Boys are about _____ to have ADD _____ girls. (twice / likely)
3. Most children are active after school. There are _____ children participating in after-school activities _____ children who don't participate at all. (five times / many)
4. On average, children with single mothers are absent from school more often. In the past 12 months, children in single-mother families missed school _____ children in two-parent families. (twice / times)

C Editing **Correct the errors. There is one error in each sentence.**

1. The incidence of respiratory allergies is twice more common in children with poor health.
2. Children in single-mother families are more likely to have learning disabilities and ADD children in two-parent families.
3. Uninsured children are more than four times likely to have unmet dental needs as children with private health insurance.
4. In families with an income of less than $35,000, the percentage of children with a learning disability is twice higher as children in families with an income of $100,000 or more.

D **Write a report on a health or education issue for a social studies class. Use at least one statistic to support your argument.**

Listening extra Time for a change

A What would you be willing to change if your partner requested it? Check (✔) the items. Add two more ideas of things you would or would not be willing to change.

- ☐ your appearance
- ☐ your job
- ☐ the way you spend your free time
- ☐ what you eat

_____

_____

B ⬇️ **Listen to Jules and Caitlin's conversation about their friend Marty. Check (✔) the topics they talk about.**

- ☐ online dating
- ☐ Marty's appearance
- ☐ being on vacation
- ☐ Marty's job
- ☐ exercise routines
- ☐ household chores
- ☐ roommates
- ☐ leaving home
- ☐ Marty's motorcycle

C ⬇️ **Listen again. Are the sentences true or false? Write T or F.**

1. The relationship between Marty and his girlfriend is going well. _____
2. Marty's girlfriend described herself accurately in her online profile. _____
3. Marty refused to change his hairstyle. _____
4. Marty used to work as a waiter, but now he works in a grocery store. _____
5. Marty has always done his own laundry. _____
6. Marty is still living with his parents. _____
7. Marty sold his motorcycle to please his girlfriend. _____
8. Both of Marty's friends are surprised at the effect Marty's girlfriend has had on him. _____

D Circle the correct options to complete the sentences.

1. Marty met his girlfriend **through a friend / on the Internet**.
2. Marty's girlfriend **is / isn't** into nature in a big way.
3. Marty is **more / less** organized than his girlfriend.
4. Marty **sometimes / never** makes dinner for himself and his girlfriend.
5. Marty's parents always dreaded him **moving back into / moving out of** their home.
6. Marty's girlfriend has changed him **slightly / completely**.

About you

E **Write about some changes you have made to your lifestyle over the years. What influenced you to make them?**

_____

_____

_____

_____

Now complete the *Unit 12 Progress chart* on page 101.   Unit 12: Psychology   **97**

Progress charts

Unit 1 Progress chart

Mark the boxes to rate your progress.
☑ I can do it.   ⚷ I can do it, but have questions.   ⚠ I need to review it.
I can . . .

	To review, go back to these pages in the Student's Book.
☐ discuss literature, reading habits, and favorite authors.	12
☐ discuss the pros and cons of reading and writing blogs.	14–15
☐ use auxiliary verbs *to, one,* and *ones* to avoid repetition.	13
☐ use 12 idioms for remembering and understanding, like *It's beyond me.*	12
☐ use stressed auxiliary verbs (*do, does*) before main verbs to add emphasis.	14
☐ use *if so* to mean "if this is true" and *if not* to mean "if this is not true."	15
☐ stress auxiliaries for emphasis.	138
☐ write a book review; link adjectives with *yet, though, if, though, if not,* or *even.*	18

Unit 2 Progress chart

Mark the boxes to rate your progress.
☑ I can do it.   ⚷ I can do it, but have questions.   ⚠ I need to review it.
I can . . .

	To review, go back to these pages in the Student's Book.
☐ discuss technology and the issue of privacy vs. security.	20
☐ evaluate the pros and cons of modern conveniences.	27
☐ add information to nouns with different types of expressions.	21
☐ use two-part conjunctions like *either . . . or* to combine ideas.	23
☐ use 12 compound adjectives like *high-speed* to describe technology.	22
☐ use adverbs like *predictably* to express what I predict or expect.	24
☐ say what is impossible with *can't / couldn't possibly.*	25
☐ use stress in noun phrases.	138
☐ write a report describing graphs, charts, and tables using expressions like *as can be seen in the graph,* etc.	28

Unit 3 Progress chart

Mark the boxes to rate your progress.
☑ I can do it.   ⚷ I can do it, but have questions.   ⚠ I need to review it.
I can . . .

	To review, go back to these pages in the Student's Book.
☐ discuss social pressures, challenges, and other new experiences.	30, 32
☐ discuss gender differences in language.	37
☐ use participle clauses to link events and add information about time or reason.	31
☐ add emphasis with *so . . . that, such . . . that, even,* and *only.*	33
☐ use at least 12 expressions with *take* (*take advantage of, take credit for*).	32
☐ use *even so* and *even then* to introduce a contrasting idea.	35
☐ use stress in expressions of contrast.	139
☐ plan and write an evaluative report; use different ways to express results.	38

Unit 4 Progress chart

Mark the boxes to rate your progress. ☑ I can do it.　☑ I can do it, but have questions.　☑ I need to review it.　I can . . .	To review, go back to these pages in the Student's Book.
☐ discuss the natural world, landscapes, and animal behavior and habitats.	42, 44
☐ consider the impact that humans have on nature.	47
☐ use future perfect forms to talk about the past in the future.	43
☐ use prepositional expressions like *as a result of* to combine ideas.	45
☐ use at least 12 expressions to describe the behavior of wildlife (*hibernate, predator*).	42
☐ use expressions like *What's more* to add and focus on new ideas.	46
☐ use *in any case* and *in any event* to strengthen arguments and reach conclusions.	47
☐ use stress in adding expressions: adding information.	139
☐ write a persuasive essay using academic prepositions (*upon, within,* etc.) and *one* for general statements.	50

Unit 5 Progress chart

Mark the boxes to rate your progress. ☑ I can do it.　☑ I can do it, but have questions.　☑ I need to review it.　I can . . .	To review, go back to these pages in the Student's Book.
☐ discuss the pros and cons of research, inventions, and innovations.	52, 54
☐ evaluate the motivation of people who are driven to perform dangerous feats.	54
☐ use adverbs with continuous and perfect forms of the passive.	53
☐ use past modals with passive forms.	55
☐ use at least 12 formal adjectives like *obsolete, portable,* adjectives into nouns (*convenient—convenience; easy—ease*).	52
☐ use expressions like *Let's put it this way* to make a point.	56
☐ use expressions like *Maybe (not), Absolutely (not), Not necessarily* in responses.	57
☐ use primary and secondary stress in expressions.	140
☐ write an opinion essay; use *it*-clauses + passive to say what people think.	60

Unit 6 Progress chart

Mark the boxes to rate your progress. ☑ I can do it.　☑ I can do it, but have questions.　☑ I need to review it.　I can . . .	To review, go back to these pages in the Student's Book.
☐ discuss business and retail; consider motivations behind shopping habits.	62, 64
☐ evaluate the benefits of online and instore shopping big and small business.	65
☐ use relative clauses that begin with pronouns or prepositions.	63
☐ use *some, any, other, others,* and *another* to refer to people and things.	65
☐ use at least 12 verbs that mean *attract* and *deter* (*entice, discourage*).	64
☐ use negative and tag questions to persuade others of your point of view.	66
☐ use *granted* to concede points.	67
☐ reduce prepositions in relative clauses.	140
☐ write a report using modal verbs to avoid being too assertive and to make recommendations.	70

Progress charts

Unit 7 Progress chart

Mark the boxes to rate your progress.

☑ I can do it.   ☐? I can do it, but have questions.   ☐! I need to review it.

I can . . .

	To review, go back to these pages in the Student's Book.
☐ discuss relationships, marriage, and family life.	74
☐ talk about the best ways to meet people.	76
☐ use conditional sentences without *if* to hypothesize.	75
☐ use *wh-* clauses as subjects and objects.	77
☐ use at least 12 expressions with *and, or, but* (*give and take*).	76
☐ use expressions like *in the end* and *in a word* to summarize or finish my points.	78
☐ use *then* to draw a conclusion from something someone said.	79
☐ write a magazine article expressing number and amount with expressions like *a number / great deal of* etc.	82

Unit 8 Progress chart

Mark the boxes to rate your progress.

☑ I can do it.   ☐? I can do it, but have questions.   ☐! I need to review it.

I can . . .

	To review, go back to these pages in the Student's Book.
☐ discuss people and events in history.	84, 86
☐ discuss the importance of history and one's family history.	89
☐ use the perfect infinitive to refer to past time.	85
☐ use cleft sentences beginning with *It* to focus on certain nouns, phrases, and clauses.	87
☐ use at least 10 adjective antonyms (*lasting—temporary; superficial—profound*).	86
☐ use expressions like *Let's not go there* to avoid talking about a topic.	88
☐ respond with *that's what I'm saying* to focus on my viewpoint.	89
☐ say perfect infinitives.	141
☐ write a narrative essay and order events in the past in different ways.	92

Unit 9 Progress chart

Mark the boxes to rate your progress.

☑ I can do it.   ☐? I can do it, but have questions.   ☐! I need to review it.

I can . . .

	To review, go back to these pages in the Student's Book
☐ discuss feats, challenges, and developments in engineering, and robots.	94, 100
☐ evaluate priorities in research and development.	99
☐ use *–ever* words to talk about unknown people or things.	95
☐ use negative adverbs (*never, not only*) + inversion to start a sentence.	97
☐ use at least 12 expressions to describe engineering projects (*erect, install*).	96
☐ use expressions like *given (that)* to introduce facts that support my opinions.	98
☐ emphasize negative phrases with *at all* and *whatsoever*.	99
☐ use fall-rise intonation for background information.	142
☐ write a classification essay; express alternatives using *rather than, as opposed to,* etc.	102

Unit 10 Progress chart

Mark the boxes to rate your progress. ☑ I can do it. ? I can do it, but have questions. ! I need to review it. I can . . .	To review, go back to these pages in the Student's Book.
☐ discuss the news, how it is reported, and if speed or accuracy is more important.	106, 111
☐ evaluate how much you trust what you hear or read in the news.	112
☐ use continuous infinitive forms to report events in progress.	107
☐ use the subjunctive to describe what should happen, what is important, and to refer to demands and recommendations.	109
☐ use at least 10 collocations with verbs and nouns (*undergo surgery*).	106
☐ highlight topics by putting them at the start or end of what I say.	110
☐ use *this* and *these* or *that* and *those* in conversation.	111
☐ use stress and intonation in longer sentences.	142
☐ summarize an article; choose singular or plural verbs.	114

Unit 11 Progress chart

Mark the boxes to rate your progress. ☑ I can do it. ? I can do it, but have questions. ! I need to review it. I can . . .	To review, go back to these pages in the Student's Book.
☐ discuss what is real and what isn't.	116, 121
☐ discuss how you would handle an emergency.	117
☐ use *be to* expressions to talk about the future.	117
☐ use passive verb complements.	119
☐ use 10 idioms with *turn* (*turn over a new leaf, turn around*).	118
☐ use expressions like *That's my concern* to express concerns.	120
☐ use *to me* to introduce an opinion.	121
☐ use stress in longer idioms.	143
☐ write an essay using academic conjunctions and expressions (*provided that, regardless of*).	124

Unit 12 Progress chart

Mark the boxes to rate your progress. ☑ I can do it. ? I can do it, but have questions. ! I need to review it. I can . . .	To review, go back to these pages in the Student's Book.
☐ discuss independence, the psychology of attraction, the brain, and stereotypes.	126, 131
☐ discuss the differences between online and in-person relationships.	128
☐ use objects + *-ing* forms after prepositions and verbs.	127
☐ use reflexive pronouns and *one another, each other*.	129
☐ use 10 new phrasal verbs (*go by, pick up on*).	128
☐ use expressions to consider different points of view and give information.	130
☐ use *to put it bluntly, mildly* etc. to indicate how I choose to express my opinions.	131
☐ use stress with reflexive pronouns.	143
☐ write a report using statistics; use expressions like *twice as likely, four times more often*.	134

Author acknowledgements

The authors would like to thank everyone who contributed material and ideas to this workbook: Guy de Villiers, Deborah Gordon, Natasha Isadora, Therese Naber, Allison Ramage, and Mary Vaughn.

Corpus

Development of this publication has made use of the Cambridge English Corpus (CEC). The CEC is a computer database of contemporary spoken and written English, which currently stands at over one billion words. It includes British English, American English and other varieties of English. It also includes the Cambridge Learner Corpus, developed in collaboration with the University of Cambridge ESOL Examinations. Cambridge University Press has built up the CEC to provide evidence about language use that helps to produce better language teaching materials.